My Lancashire Childhood

CATHERINE ROTHWELL

SUTTON PUBLISHING

First published in 1993
by Owl Books

This revised and expanded edition
first published in 2007 by
Sutton Publishing Limited · Phoenix Mill
Thrupp · Stroud · Gloucestershire · GL5 2BU

British Library Cataloguing in Publication Data
A catalogue record for this book is available from the British Library

ISBN 978-07509-4866-1

Title page photograph
*My brothers Charles and Edward, born in the last two years of the First World
War. They were great companions, but as different as chalk and cheese. Charles
was quiet, thoughtful and gentle and Edward was rebellious and mischievous.
This photograph was taken in the back yard of the family home, a railway cottage
at 39 Newtown Street, Heaton Park.*

ACKNOWLEDGEMENTS

I am indebted to Lancashire Library and Manchester Polytechnic for
allowing me to use two photographs. Also to Stanley Butterworth;
Bob Gibson; John R. Houghton; Kathleen Hall Houghton;
John Charles Houghton; Edward Houghton; Eric Mills; Ron Severs;
Ron Loomes; Lytham Heritage Group; Barbara Strachan.

Typeset in 11/12pt Photina.
Typesetting and origination by
Sutton Publishing Limited.
Printed and bound in England.

Contents

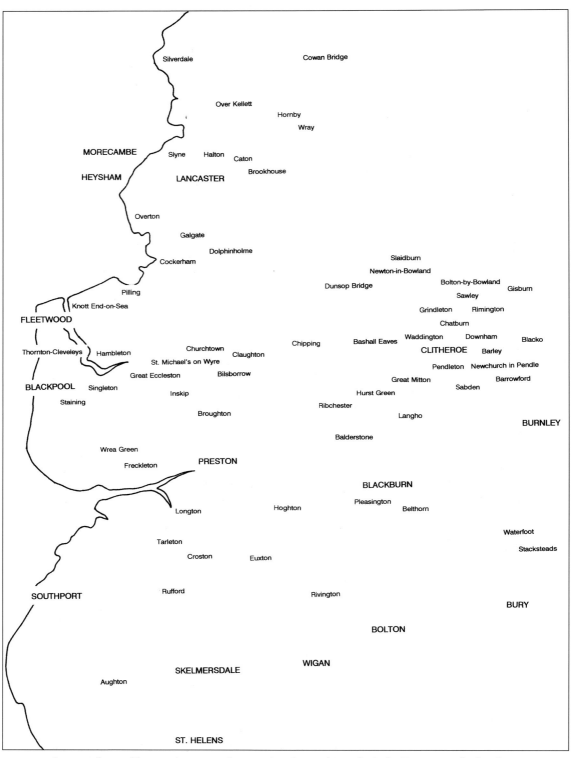

A map of our old stamping grounds, covering Lancashire, the Lake District and what has now become Merseyside. (Map by Ron Loomes)

Introduction

In the 1920s and early '30s when most of the following impressions were formed it was difficult to get work. A typical joke of the period described one of the great number of unemployed hearing cries of distress as he walked along the canal bank, and hurrying to see a man struggling in the water.

'Where do you work?' queried the man on the towpath and on being told, raced off to that address leaving the man to drown.

'One of your men has been drowned in the cut,' he said. 'I've come for his job.'

'Too late – the man who pushed him in has got it.'

'Doctors' wives die and cobblers' children go barefoot' were other cynicisms at the time. In recent years these have been levelled at me for not sorting out my own family tree but helping others to do theirs. The closest relations which my brother and I best recalled fleetingly are in the rudimentary family tree that follows, if such it can be termed. But we were nonetheless interested in the shadowy, unrecorded past and the characters who peopled it, people whom we had never met. Indeed, in some ways these seemed the more intriguing. In childhood, the sensations, sights, sounds, smells are inseparable to be soaked up like a sponge; many experiences apparently lying dormant until perhaps years later they are triggered off to suddenly surface with a feeling of deja vu. Rather than the stereotyped family tree, a collection of impressions seemed preferable, the deepest being expressed in photographs all of which are linked with a Lancashire childhood.

The new edition of *My Lancashire Childhood* is dedicated to my parents Clement and Ethel, and is written for my grandchildren; so there are moments in the account when history and anecdote intervene and are not truly 'my' childhood. They are, however, so closely woven into my early life so inexorably and insistently, ancestral voices calling, that towards the end of my own long life I make no excuse for their inclusion.

Edward Hoghton of Belthorn and Yate & Pickup Bank, Darwen, was innkeeper of the Dog Inn. (It is interesting to note from indentures that Hoghton became Houghton on the advice of some lawyer at some indeterminate date. Two versions of the family name caused legal concern.)

The first Edward had several properties besides the inn, i.e. a row of cottages, two farms, a butcher's shop and a small, early, cotton textile mill in which in that inventory of his possessions the machinery is stated to be

The Hoghton family in the 1890s. This photograph, the oldest we have, shows Uncle William holding the kettle, great-great-grandmother, Annie Hoghton (William's wife), opposite, and my father Clement standing beside the swing. The occasion is a picnic in the garden at either Belthorn or Downham. The family photographs in this book were taken by Clement using his large, heavy-plate camera which he made himself, on a wooden tripod, draped with a black cloth.

'very old'. It is recorded that an occupant of one of his cottages filled the interstices between the millstone grit flagstones on the parlour floor with lead, so that he might enjoy long, uninterrupted rocking in his chair.

Edward worshipped in the Established Church at Haslingden Grane but later in the 1880s they attended Emmanuel Church, Oswaldtwistle, where members of the family are buried under a worn, thin headstone of white Carrara marble, while Clement occupies a new grave alone. On the South wall of Emmanuel is a jewel-glowing, stained glass window dedicated to Edward. The Hoghtons and the local Belthorn clergyman had a bitter disagreement over something ('I hold with the headmaster, right or wrong.') Such outrageous talk to a Hoghton would damn the cleric for ever, yet they were loyal to the Establishment. Grandmother Catherine raised her brolly to the statue of Disraeli in Ormskirk Market Place shouting above costermongers' cries: 'Good old Dizzy.' William Ewart Gladstone was set down by great grandfather 'Ned' as 'Bloody Billy' over the General Gordon affair at Khartoum, yet as a child I distinctly remember a marble bust of the great statesman at the old family house. Like the de Hoghtons who helped to build places of worship and enjoyed a true catholicity in their circle of friends, the Belthorn Hoghtons stoutly believed in tolerance for all.

The eldest son of the eldest son was always christened Edward, another of that name being known as The Dancer since he excelled in the pastime.

He left a son Edward and a daughter Elizabeth Agnes, neither physically strong. The son probably suffered from hypothermia since his habit was to sit in front of a roaring fire. Folks nearby could smell his clothes scorching in the heat. One day this Edward's hat and dashing clothes arrived in a big tin trunk together with all sorts of other paraphernalia. The hat of superfine black felt could be folded up. Edward must have resembled Giuseppe Verdi when wearing it. My brothers loved dressing up as pirates in this garb and there was an exquisite beaded silk bodice for me. We all thrilled at these mysterious items with their romantic whiffs from the past but Mother was hurt, knowing that they had descended on defenceless poor relations as items to be got rid of.

Catherine Cronshaw refused to marry Edward until he got rid of the Dog Inn, deciding that an innkeeper could not make a desirable husband. To his two sons caught swimming in the mill dam the erstwhile innkeeper was reported to have said, 'Wait until your mother hears of this' – indicative of who wore the trousers in that Victorian household, and it is a sad fact that with the parting of the old inn began the salting away of the rest of the Hoghton property.

Jonathan Cronshaw, Catherine's first husband, could not have been a poor man. Two articles of furniture I recall would have pleased Arthur

Jonathan Cronshaw Houghton, Blackburn Market Inspector (far left) was an uncle I never knew. He died in the prime of life from typhoid fever after eating mussels. His hobby was collecting antiques and paintings. I recall that he managed to acquire a David Cox watercolour at a reasonable price, a Venetian vase and a set of Spode china among other lovely items.

Negus: a mahogany long case clock and a walnut inlaid William and Mary bureau of superfine cabinet work. Unfortunately all Clement Houghton's possessions at the year of his death, 1954, fell into the hands of his elder brother whom Clement, in a moment of great weakness, had named his executor. These and the many works of art collected by Clement's brother Jonathan, who died of typhoid fever after eating mussels, were lost to our family forever and the house sold for a song.

Catherine had a half sister Polly who revelled in late nights, entertainment, trips to Blackpool, Bolton and Wigan by charabanc, not to mention hot pie, cow heel and chip suppers. In the 1930s Polly graduated to weekend trips to the Continent, indulging in the same fare. Her rather low tastes must have been a trial to Catherine who, I suspect, was a snob. Certainly Polly was jolly whereas Catherine was perpetually disapproving.

A solid-gold watch and a beautifully carved, long-handled parasol of silk were among Catherine's personal possessions.

> How sweet my childhood days were,
> How merry and free . . .

This from one of Catherine's poems which has survived.

Widowed for the second time, Catherine and her son Clement, who both disliked the country, escaped to Blackburn to a double-fronted house in Brantfell Road. Queen's Park was a favourite retreat.

Clement married Ethel Fielden, our mother, whose father was a master baker from Rossendale. Mother's grandmother, Grandma Worswick, had a

Mother, who rarely sat down, had a hard, wooden chair with a plywood seat. 'Lady Hornby', an upholstered Chesterfield, was reserved for Father but, already having seen better days, it expired in a groan of springs and kapok on the night the marble fireplace fell on it. Luckily we were all in bed but the soot from the chimney wrecked the room.

general store on Burnley Road which then carried the monopoly for Cadbury's chocolate in the whole valley. I remember her daughter Emma with shiny, auburn hair well into old age. Grandad Worswick, described as the 'please yourself sort', sailed twice to USA when it was an adventure. On returning home the second time for more money from the shop till, he insisted on the whole family embracing the Shaker sect which was founded by a lady in Manchester, an early feminist who believed the Holy Ghost was

Above: Even as small children we loved walking on the moors where mother spent her childhood. This is Pye's Farm in snow. The bleak Pennines in all weathers became part of our growing-up years.

Emma Worswick was our maternal grandmother and here she is in her best hat, photographed by my father in his Waterfoot Studio. As a girl she had lovely Titian red hair and wore small pieces of good jewellery. She considered Lancashire comedians to be 'vulgar'. By the way she pronounced it you knew what she meant. She also had no time at all for the grammar schools. I fell from grace the moment I won a scholarship.

This group of young men, the Jolly Ollies, entertained in Lancashire villages in 1908.
Some of those included in this photograph are Tom Bradley, Walter Billington, Sid Boden,
Bert Yates, Edwin Rothwell, Bob Bush, Harry Hilton and J. Brown. A favourite booking
was Thursday market day, when they bought hand-raised pork pies from Singleton's
famous shop on the High Street, Garstang. Grandad Rothwell never forgot those pies! The
men are seen here outside Worden Park.

of her sex. It was flourishing in the 1850s in the States, the men of the
movement wearing aprons or 'brats' while the women wore plain dresses and
white bonnets like the early Quakers. Grandfather Fielden differed. Seeing the
band of the Salvation Army approaching, he roared to the world at large,
'There goes Salvation' and, smiting his breast, 'Here goes damnation.'
Grandad Worswick, obviously a born ecumenical leader, played the violin in
the gallery of the Methodist Church and at choir sermons was happy to play
in the Anglican Church and at choir sermons was happy to play in the
Anglican building of Newchurch. That was the time of the famous Dean
Layrocks, whose singing fame spread far and wide beyond Pendle Hill.

Father's 'side' for some obscure reason seemed to consider themselves
superior clay, but what we children could never forgive was that they were
not nice to Mother. Her side of the family, more human and likeable, was
visited by boarding 'Puffing Billy' at Bury railway station and chugging
along the rural line through Summerseat, Stubbins and Edenfield. Charlie
had his favourite sweetmeat, a raisin bar, while I sucked away at my delight,
a small bar of Fry's Cream Chocolate. We were with Mother and thus we
were happy and she was happy too. For a short while she was going home.

Catherine Rothwell, Poulton

CHAPTER ONE

The Railway Children

The wall was a rock garden; it was part of our playground and it was also a grand stand for viewing the passing trains. Daily, except Sunday, throughout the year we were on the wall at half-past seven in the evening, standing or sitting, waiting for the loaded coal train to pass up the incline. In early childhood I sat there, supported by Mother's arm, my elder brother (by six years) standing beside me. Later, aided by the height of the dustbin, I declined Mother's help, and a little later still I climbed the wall using the crannies as toe holds. 'Driver, driver', shouted my brother, while I, giving support to the fireman, called loudly for his favoured attention. Every evening we stood there waving. Only absence from home, illness or inclement weather prevented our attendance. But, as the years passed we no longer shouted, merely waved and, finally came the evening when even that was too much. Thereafter we no longer watched, we had grown older and wiser in the ways of the world.

As little children this routine was anticipated: after it we were washed and went to bed, but five minutes before the train was due we were waiting, heads turned to the left from which direction we should see the first billow of smoke rising from the long tunnel. Steadily climbing and rounding the curve, the thunderous blast of the exhaust was joy to our ears and the pungency of mingled steam and burning coal sheer pleasure to our noses. From the tall smoke stack the shower of red-hot grit was flung high into the air, amidst the belching black smoke and momentarily white vapour. This awesome sight was enhanced by the mad racing of the driving wheels as they failed to grip the rails from time to time, and at this the red sparks would fountain higher above the billowing wake. Thod-thod, thod-thod went the following trucks, and often the screech from a locking brake-shoe, and the judder, judder, judder as the brake handle beat wildly up and down under the inexorable pull of the locomotive. On winter nights with rain we still watched through the kitchen window. Our heroes, standing under the shelter of tarpaulin sheet slung from the edge of the cab canopy, chuffed by on their iron monster, and the red glare from the open firebox door was a friendly island of light in the fretting waters of surrounding darkness.

By the four acres of land over that wall we watched the march of the seasons. On the opposite side of the cutting was a wild service tree, and

We loved the 'softly panting train' so much we could have been called the Railway Children. On summer Wakes Week holiday, staying in Blackpool in lodgings overlooking Central station, Edward could not be coaxed from the 'digs'. He spent all of his time watching the trains arriving and departing.

when a green mist surrounded the bare branches we knew that spring had arrived, just as we were certain of Whitsuntide when the sickly pink rhododendrons flowered. A patch of helianthus also sprang up in summer, and I for one, found its odour strange and disturbing. Surpassing all these were the privets that had been left untended, and growing unchecked to a height of nine or ten feet, became a mass of creamy white fragrance in early July. I have several times heard it said that privet blossom is offensive smelling, but its heady, never-forgotten tang is beloved of the humble bee. After all these years whenever I catch a stray whiff of privet, or see the flowers turning brown on their stalks lying in a shallow pool of rain on an August pavement the days of childhood are evoked. The scent is bitter-sweet.

To the left the wall ran, by a series of rising courses, beneath a row of black poplar trees whose leaves were plagued by caterpillars in summer. Beyond these trees stood a large wooden shed, at one time a firelighter factory, and at another a garage, with a solitary pump proclaiming Pratt's petrol. The building was patched with cast-off enamelled steel plates bearing past and present advertisements: Stuart Horizontal Engines, Stephen's Ink, Cherry Blossom Boot Polish, Benson's Watches. One's nose was titillated by the smells that clung to the building: lubricating fluid with its overtones of castor oil, naphthalene always, and creosote in the slow,

As the first girl in the family, I had to be named after my paternal grandmother, who, in return, bequeathed to me her long gold chain and solid gold watch. In this photograph I am wearing an outfit knitted all in green wool by Aunt Annie Ward. I liked it, even the enveloping hat because green was and still is my favourite colour.

quiet hours of a hot Saturday afternoon. In winter mist seemed to drift round the place, harsh, hostile and sour with soot.

And yet there was the wall, and over it, the railway cutting, and the fall of the year; there was the stone edge of the long paths of amber light reflected from the distant signals; there was the hot, sweet smell of lamp oil, and the shuttered guide lamp that fluttered blue in the rising wind before turning to a yellow steadiness, and there was the never-ceasing moan of the telegraph wires, the insistent rattle of a wantonly-swinging gate, and the faraway whistle of an engine.

The street was quite short beginning at the railway bridge, where it changed its name, and ascended an incline with stone setts all the way, to help the poor dray horses we were told. Buff gritstone pavements bordered it with worn flags and smooth kerbs not much higher than the carriageway itself. At the lower end where our terraced cottage stood, but four doors away, was a gas lamp and the maker's mark was the sign of a crab; the lamplighter's son went to my school. This four-sided lantern crowned with a copper cap was fitted with glass trapdoors. Through these the lamplighter thrust his long staff surmounted with a brass cylinder and bearing a pilot light. As he pushed over the wing tap there was a loud pop and the twin mantles flamed into a greenish-yellow glare. Only at nightfall in the darker months could I, like R.L. Stevenson, wait for my Leary* from the parlour window, for in summer the lanterns were collected, and conveyed to the Town's Yard on what appeared at casual sight to be a ladder of wood mounted on a hand cart, each lantern placed upright between each two rungs.

---

* Robert Louis Stevenson, poet and author, refers to the lamp lighter of his childhood as 'Leary'.

A few yards further on, in the middle of the road, was the barred grating of a manhole, and we children were bidden never to stand over or near it 'because of the bad air'. We did though, at times, since the sound of falling water below our feet fascinated us. From where did the water come and to whence did it flow? Only later did we learn about sewers.

On the opposite side of the street I remember three things among others: the sandy foundations of the railway bridge and the cutting with hundreds of blue lupins in summer; a tall laburnum tree, and a run of old-fashioned roses, like a white Dorothy Perkins. Next came a Congregational Chapel in a half an acre, surrounded by a palisade of upturned railway sleepers and partly by an incomplete brick wall. Gossip said that this place of worship had been built against the wishes of the Lord of the Manor. During one of his absences, for he had properties elsewhere, his agent had sold the land to the chapel sponsors and the building was a fait accompli when the noble gentleman returned. He never forgave the trustees. One can quite believe this story for it is well known that he cost the railway company a pretty penny when they wished to cross his land in the early years of the railway age, for he insisted that the line should only be allowed if it passed beneath his private park, and tunnelling through sand can prove very awkward. Before we children became regular attenders at the Established Church we went to the Sunday school opposite, and occasionally attended Morning Service in the chapel on the floor above. There was a wide spiral staircase with stained glass windows of floral patterns, and at the top a heavy curtain, sign of bourgeois comfort against draught, shrouded the door. The minister wore striped trousers and a frock coat, white shirt with stiffened front and cuffs and a grey silk necktie. He had also a silk hat, spats over kid leather buttoned boots and pince-nez spectacles. He was the essence of dignity, and to me as a small child he impressed far more than the pink-faced, tubby Anglican priest I was later to meet, who never seemed to take off his cassock unless to don an alb, amice, chasuble and all the rest of the High Church gear.

At the top of the street, one on either side stood corner shops: on the right a tripe shop and on the left a fried fish shop.

The tripe shop had originally been a private dwelling, last one of a terrace facing the main road, and the window of the front room still carried its original six panes. Some shops never got beyond this stage but were kept limited in size. A house doing baking only, rather than a baker's shop, was quite popular then, often run by a widow left in impecunious straits, a cottage industry doing nothing beyond baking bread and teacakes, and a cushion against hard times. For several years I helped to collect the bread and delicious bread it was, baked in the coal oven of a cottage kitchen range.

A solitary woman served in the tripe shop: never was I served by another person. No food was ever displayed in the window. Instead two or three pot plants filled the space, resting on a floor of plain tiles. Behind the plants a discreet gingham check curtain, gathered on a tensed cord and supported by small wooden posts at the extremities, hung down, the whole about eighteen inches high. One entered, and the bell, clanged by the striker attached to the opening top edge of the door, brought out the shopwoman, dour and middle-aged.

'Yes?'

'A pound of best seam tripe, please,' placing the money on the narrow, high counter, just above a child's eye-level. While the meat was cut, so white and almost odourless one looked at the pictures on the opposite wall, those one had seen so many times before, a pair of strongly coloured prints depicting various breeds of parrots.

'Here you are.'

'Thank you.'

Another clang and one was out again descending to the pavement by three semicircular steps.

The fried fish shop opposite had a bigger trade, noisier, more talkative (since one had to wait) and more bustling. The owner and his wife ceaselessly plied their daily trade without ever seeming to rest or take holiday. Both had that well-tubbed, well-scrubbed look, and both were clad in spotless white overalls. The anthem sung in the choir seemed to refer to them,

> What are these that are arrayed in white robes
> And whence came they?

Here I must interpolate that in the times and places of which I write this creed of soapsuds, in a practical rather than literal sense, this much-scrubbing of bare woodwork seemed always to be taking place somewhere in the week. Pails of hot water, blocks of wire-cut Windsor pale primrose and blue mottled soap and reddened wet arms to the elbow, were sure to be seen in some food shop. The faint smell of citronella oil could often be detected before the week was out whether at the butcher's, with sawdust underfoot, or at the baker's (they scrubbed early), the fishmonger's (he scrubbed late), or the greengrocer (he was erratic and worked on a movable feast).

The proprietor and his wife moved to and fro before the chip range like officiating priests at the sacrificial altar dedicated to the god of the belly. At intervals the man would tend his twin coal fires from opposite ends, and into the pans of boiling fat resting above those fires, would thrust a wire skimmer shallowly catching the fragments of charring chip bits. Again, he would grasp a chip, drawn to the surface in a wire cage, and test it between right finger and thumb for readiness. Less frequently a pail of whole peeled potatoes was forced through a steel chip machine by hand into a white enamelled colander below. Everyone ate fish on Tuesday and/or Friday in that area, Catholic or no, and consequently one could purchase a fish piece covered in golden batter for small cost. These also the man prepared carefully and then floated into the heaving, swirling fat. So, timed almost to the nearest second this frying routine continued throughout the day, apart from a brief rest in the afternoon, never hurried, never at a loss for something to do.

His wife sold and wrapped the food and helped the children who asked for 'Plenty of salt and vinegar, please' from a giant aluminium salt shaker and a porcelain-corked vinegar bottle. It was possible to sit and eat one's purchases at the cast iron, marble topped tables, indeed, for another 1d; one could make the meal a feast with a helping of boiled, parched peas, perching before it on a wooden stool; but when we called we were generally on our way home, and sit we never did.

Secured to the outside wall of the shop was a 1914–1918 street roll of honour, illuminated in vellum and fixed into a hardwood frame surrounded by a latin cross, and bearing the names of men who joined the services but who never returned to their homes in that street. For King and Country read the title, In Proud Memory. Other streets, too, had their memorials in a similar design, but before I was ten years old the majority of these cenotaphs had disappeared.

Behind the tripe shop stood a courtyard surrounded by two-up-and-two-down artisans' cottages, the space cobbled completely and entered by a gateway set in the front elevation of two adjoining houses. This was Gartside's Court. Another court, designated to the lower status of alley, and whitewashed all round to a height of eight feet, stood nearby. This area was generally avoided by my friends and me because of the rough boys who lived there. Upper rooms were reached from outside stone steps. Perhaps they had originally been weavers' homes, for their age showed in the stone floors – I was invited there once and had a cup of tea, from a most elegant cup and saucer – in the roofing tiles of Pennine sandstone and simple V wooden gutters. The courtyard of the alley was cobbled in a similar way to the court, and I seem to remember a pump standing in one corner.

The only other building I knew well was Fred Jackson's grocery store and off-licence, more the latter than the former, though he did a fair trade in commodities and it was for these I made my visits. It stood halfway up the slight hill. It seems a little strange now that so many different proprietary brands of soap products were for sale, and not just the brand names of two or three limited manufacturers. There was Brook's Monkey Brand, a scouring block for scullery use; there was Ivy soap – 'It floats'; and Dr Lovelace's soap. Acdo block was cut in wafers for Monday's washing and Gossage's Beefeater Carbolic was kept by the kitchen sink for casual washing. All these in addition to those we still have, excepting the Hedley (later Procter and Gamble products) which did not meet the eye in our parts until just before 1936. Jackson's had a complete glass cupboard (formerly stocking a well-known brand of chocolate from the Big Three, Cadbury's, Fry's and Rowntree's) and it held many proprietary medicines to which the poorer off resorted for relief in sickness. However much the present National Health arrangements are full of shortcomings they are infinitely better than the woefully inadequate 'provisions' of the 1920s.

Sam and Emma Briggs were local shopkeepers and friends of my parents, 1890s.

Then one went 'on the box' only in dire necessity; hospital was feared and side-stepped as far as one possibly could do so, and when regrettably and unavoidably it could not be averted the sufferer had to haggle with a petty official on the price he could afford to pay in that institution before he was allowed over the threshold. Consequently, the lowest-paid workers clung to faith in the power of manufacturing pharmaceutical chemists. How great the contrast between the poor and their local Member of Parliament, when they occasionally read in their local free press that he was being treated in a London nursing home for a minor ailment.

Throughout the year there were itinerant vendors of small-value goods: hawkers and door-to-door salesmen, keen after patronage, however trifling. One man comes immediately to mind since he came regularly every fortnight, year after year, but for three seasons of the year only, summer being excepted. He wore a cotton union shirt without collar in lieu of which he wore a white, fringed silk muffler, which also helped to dispense with a necktie. A dark woollen overcoat over a blue serge suit covered him and on his head he had a check cloth cap. His hands were large, white and strong and had a most capable look about them. He carried a large rectangular wicker basket, a baker's basket, well-filled with crumpets and

Ted Gleeson and Bert Hackinsall in charge of Hodgkinson's float in a carnival procession. Hodgkinson's, a mineral water firm, produced fizzy drinks, soda water siphons, sasparilla and other herbal drinks.

freshly-made, limp oatcakes, the whole decently covered with a white linen cloth. When it rained the basket wore a hat of black oilskin mackintosh gathered round the edges with elastic.

Every Monday passed by the 'sambone' man. That was the two-note call he seemed to enunciate walking alongside his small, light cart drawn by a donkey, with the woollen rags he preferred piled at the front high up and the rear of the cart low down, weighed there by the burden of white, cream and brown stones used to smarten outside steps. These he traded for rags or desirable rubbish or junk.

On Mondays, too, came the clothes-prop man with unmusical call and four or five wooden clothes props for the washing line for sale.

The ice cream man from whose cart, pushed by hand, we were allowed to buy our two penny and one penny cornets lived in the street. Of a multitude of hokey-pokey men his barrow alone had an English name, and unlike the rest it was soberly painted and carried none of the fanciful scenes from an improbable mythology with festoons and cupids simpering at each corner. He was a tubby little fellow, and certainly worked for his money, pushing the heavy barrow mile after mile. The apron he wore was spotlessly white and

The rag and bone ('sambone') man with a donkey and cart. He would be seen calling out in the street for 'any old rags, jars, bottles, rabbit skins and old chairs to mend'. The rag and bone man paid with 'donkey stones', cream and brown, which women used to colour cleaned hearth stones, steps and the pavement in front of their houses. The Flying Dutchman Inn is also seen here, for sale, in the 1870s.

so starched that the hem stood out from his body, not following his plump contours. It was quite as large as a baker's apron and had a capacious cash pocket, which, surely, could never have been full. I never saw him once without his cap while he was selling though I did know he had a bald head.

Once every summer came the herb seller bearing a large brown basket of sage and thyme. Once or twice I can remember he brought forward lavender in small bunches for the linen chest.

There was a haberdasher person – it could be a man or a woman – carrying round a large fibre suitcase full of cards of pearl and cloth faced buttons; sewing cotton and button cotton; cards of darning wool and knicker elastic, hair nets, boot and shoe laces and needles and pins in paper; narrow machine-made laces and trimmings besides many other different items to such a degree that one would wonder how on earth could they fit into such a container!

Mr Bulmer, a country postman, is seen here on his rounds, 1893.

The milkman who came each morning daily changed his tactics in summer when he also came in the early evening, when one could enjoy a good cup of tea if perchance the morning's milk had turned sour in the thunderous weather – no refrigerators for the working class in those days! He looked the horsey type and wore riding breeches, brown leather gaiters and a hacking jacket of woollen check. The graceful milk float, drawn by a chestnut horse generally carried two milk churns on one side and a large cylindrical, nickel-plated milk tank of a far greater capacity, at least twenty gallons, I should say, on the other. This tank was fitted with a close-fitting lid beneath which, inside, two metal measures with crooked handles hung, not touching the liquid for the tank was never more than half full. A line of milk kits of differing sizes hung by their brass clips from the rail inside the float, stamped with the imperial measure and the owner's name. After he had measured the desired quantity one collected the milk at the door in an appropriate jug. By arrangement, though not as a general sale, he sold eggs and cream.

The seasons were known by their games, played in the Little Back behind the terrace, or, in summer, in the street itself, or one which was at right angles to it. In tender childhood these games were all gentle: bowling hoops, whip and top, hopscotch, hide and seek, and skipping – this with a length of vegetable rope we had begged at the greengrocer's from off the boxes of Spanish oranges, thirteen for a bob, that entered the country about December. These games were generally played in the cooler seasons. Others:

Ghost in the Garden, Buckets and Strides, Sly Fox, Old Woman of Botany Bay, and, surely, marbles were less active and therefore more suitable for warmer weather. Later, when the girls withdrew to play only with members of their own sex, the boys ganged together in Kick Can and Rally-O Relieve O, games that never seemed to finish, that were better played at night and which involved much running and calling from street to street. In winter, too, each boy made himself a winter warmer which consisted of an empty four-ounce cocoa tin in which a nail was used to punch several holes in the lid. Inside, a piece of smouldering cotton waste was inserted and by judicious blowing one could produce a fair amount of heat and a great deal of smelly smoke. On the earth surface of Little Back the girls at play would scrape house interiors with a pointed stick drawing, in a stylised manner the things they would expect to find in their house. Alas, they all drew pots of gay pelargoniums on every windowsill (I can't remember any in that street), and proudly on the first floor appeared an elegant bathroom (which no house possessed) with an inner lavatory pan (when all the street had to retire outside).

We made liquorice water, alias Spanish juice. A four ounce or slightly larger medical flat bottle was fitted with a cork and filled with water into which small pieces of hard liquorice were added, and the bottle rested in a warm place between vigorous shakings. After a day the mixture was thick, brown and frothy and in this state was imbibed, if not with joy, then with satisfaction. Sweets seemed harder to come by in those days than they are to the average child now. As a special concession, since Charles was in the choir, my parents allowed him 'singing toffee', limited to a halfpenny a week, and there seemed to be a great variety of choice with such slender means at one's disposal. Imagine asking for a ha'porth of fat ducks, green peas and new potatoes, and getting some of each in a triangular shaped bag!

CHAPTER TWO

Watch the Birdie!

I was brought up with the scent of retouching fluid and Hypo developer in my nostrils. When Father was not guillotining and mounting photographs in the large kitchen before a roaring coal fire, round which we all gathered, he would be in his dark room in one of the cellars, or tinkering with his enlarger in a shrouded parlour. The scent of the chemicals hung in the air, mingling with the aroma of Lancashire hot pot.

As there were roving reporters there were in the early 1900s roving photographers. I certainly recall from birth and at close hand a moving kaleidoscope of five and a half inch by three and a half inch postcards appearing and disappearing the whole year round. Subjects caried according to season. Whitsuntide Walks resulted in dozens of silk banners, white-clad girls carrying baskets of flowers, Boys' Brigades, bandsmen, Girl Guides and ministers from all the churches.

Within days Father had these postcards developed, glossed and mounted on a large display board in the front room window. Each one had a number incised in the corner. Customers would gaze, knock at our front door which opened onto the street and request the number they wanted. Very occasionally the number would be 'fogged' and therefore the photo unavailable, which caused some disappointment. I cannot remember how much each one cost other than that they were a few coppers in old money.

We had three pieces of studio furniture: a tottering bamboo plant stand; a grandiose chaise-longue used for adults in their Sunday-best clothes and a high-backed, blue-upholstered oak chair with barley sugar stick shaped spindles which children clung to (children holding tennis rackets, or clad in Confirmation dresses or sailor suits). At the front of the chair, plump babies were sat on an even plumper cushion. As Dad used magnesium flash light, when the 'gun' went off, eyes widened and jaws dropped, resulting in stunned looks or worse still open mouths, so subjects usually went through the ordeal twice. He once set the curtains on fire, terrifying patrons and the whole household.

How I wish I had his street scenes! People liked to assemble with neighbours in front of their lace curtains or stand on scrubbed, cream-stoned steps, in the window the aspidistra plant placed to full advantage. Usually taken in summer, 'Holly Street', 'Newtown Street', 'Wilton Street' etc. was carefully scratched onto the gelatinous coating of the glass

A portrait of a mother and child taken in a typical studio.

When a photographer appeared in the streets long ago it was such a novelty that anyone around wanted to be in the picture. This image dates from the days when my father was a young man moving his heavy camera, folding tripod, black cloth and even his makeshift darkroom around with him.

negative, faithfully to identify the print. I realise now that there were some lovely ones of children playing games: marbles, whip and top, skipping, bowling hoops. Again the display would go up and people purchased, often to send off to friends or relatives who might never have seen their houses or the new baby. 'Best Wishes', 'Christmas Greetings', 'Happy Birthday' were often printed on the backs of these postcards. All photographic supplies came from the Kentmere factory at Staveley, then in Westmorland, and I remember anxious conferences between my parents when prices went up.

School classes, carnivals, town pageants, the soldiers at Ashton-under-Lyne and Bury Barracks and in the huts at Heaton Park were all subjects taken on a regular basis. When trade slackened, Dad took himself off to Wales or Blackpool to photograph the crowds there, improvising some truly ingenious dark rooms. There was one at Holyhead that had been a ship's galley. It was sited in a junk yard guarded by a fierce black dog called Dragon, a dog that lived up to its name.

When Dad tried out a reflex camera designed and constructed entirely by himself we children were guinea pigs. Greater action and flexibility was possible with this camera, my eldest brother being thrilled to use it for bird photography. Father, who hoped to patent his invention, procured tiny brass plates engraved 'The Paxman Camera Company' to be screwed onto the camera, but he never had the money to make his dream a reality.

One of my father's commissions was to photograph school classes. This early Standard VI Girls' class was 'produced under the patronage of the School Board'.

My friend Fred Woods,
photographed on Fleetwood
beach not far from his home.
Fred became quite famous
and even met the Queen in
later life.

Following his instructions my sister and I ran down lanes, scaled walls, climbed rocks, leap-frogged energetically and languished amidst flowers, sometimes damaging clothes in the process, but it was all in the cause of progress and art.

Every event was recorded, even the street's May Queen. On holidays the heavy plate camera with its ponderous, wooden tripod and large, black cloth drape was always in the background (shades of donkey rides, sea immersions and charabanc jaunts). It was small wonder that I grew up with a passion for old photographs and a magpie instinct for collecting nostalgic postcards. I often wonder whatever happened to those hundreds of postcards sold from our two up, two down terraced house. A few family pictures remain but the rest of them must be knocking around at postcard conventions. I have never had the luck to find a single one. Perhaps going back to my 'roots', trawling junk shops and car boot sales might reap rich rewards, but could I bear the memories?

I am rather proud now to have been connected with the roving photographer's trade but at the time it all passed blissfully over my head. Bent on my own pursuits, I was completely unaware of the valuable social chronicle building up around me. If only the glass negatives had been saved! They were so little prized at the time that one boy used them for target practice in the long attic above his father's chemist's shop.

The photographs in the Introduction and other chapters of Mother, Grandmother and we children were taken by my father, Clement Houghton.

CHAPTER THREE

Market Days Remembered

Market days! Oh, the sights, sounds and smells of those long-ago occasions! Jostling farmers in leather gaiters, their wives clad in starched aprons and floppy sun bonnets; scurrying villagers anxious to buy the freshest and cheapest produce; sharp-eyed lads hanging around the toffee apple stall! Sounds? The clatter of horses' hooves and clang of iron-shod wheels as carts edged as close as possible to unload.

Market Street, Chorley, where one of my favourite markets was held in the days when I searched for antiques and old photographs – a good hunting ground.

A Victorian market staged in Fylde, 2000.

The loud ringing of the market bell allowed trading to commence. Pervading all was the scent of horseflesh, leather harness and the tang of fresh-pulled vegetables especially in autumn when celery-hearts, beetroots, carrots, parsnips, savoy cabbage, kohlrabi were piled high, earth still fresh upon them. A pungent mingling of manure, straw and sacking titillated nostrils and amidst this hurly burly the knife-grinder furiously treadled his machine, causing sparks to fly. That set the dogs barking.

Even as far back as the twelfth century market days were held at crossroads, on village greens, in the shadow of church walls, even in the churchyard itself. From these, shops evolved, so it is not surprising that such a long tradition rouses distinct nostalgia. Next to the church, the market was the most important institution, the very hub of country life, where friendships were made, old scores settled and deals struck by a handshake.

In mind's eye I still see the lines of patient horses waiting to be sold, big boys hanging around hoping to be hired to lead a stallion to one of a score of farms in the vicinity of our medieval town, Poulton-le-Fylde.

On 'flesh days' before Christmas stalls were laden from end to end of Market Place, with portions of pigs, sides of beef, saddles of lamb, coops of live chickens. The symbolic Yule loaf was baked and given to housewives. Candles, hand-made in moulds, were also given, but the old custom of apprentices shooting at lighted candles set in turnips by the Market Cross had died out.

A horse sale held in Market Square, Poulton, in the early years of the twentieth century.

The stocks and market cross at Poulton-le-Fylde.

For the farmers who had to travel miles over the Moss, market day started before sun up. With the farmer's wife riding pillion and heavy panniers to carry, pity the poor horse. Heavy wagons piled high with country produce lumbered down rutted lanes. A further hazard lay in fording the River Wyre. This had to coincide with low tide so time was of the essence. With such a scramble to get across, 'ford rage' resulted in overturned carts.

Winter days brought added excitement tinged with fear as kerosene lamps clamped to stalls glowed and hissed and rain dripped from the protective tarpaulin sheets. I clung fiercely to Mother's hand as we forged our way to the lady on Bury Market who sold nothing but eggs, butter and cheese. Everything about her was spotless, her stall an oasis in the fretting darkness.

When farms disappeared and market days degenerated into displays of clothes, pots and utensils the zest and variety of the 1900s disappeared for ever. The glory departed.

CHAPTER FOUR

Farms & Shops

Among the farms were Houseman's in Carr Head Lane, Hodgkinson's at the bottom of the Breck opposite the old railway station, Roskell's near Poulton Curve station and Stirzaker's at Manor Farm, Mains Lane. Mr and Mrs Hull ran a black and white timbered farm in Argyle Road, their pastures extending to where Garstang road now throbs with traffic. Frank Nicholson conducted his business as a cattle dealer from his farm in Hardhorn and was to be seen regularly at Poulton Auction Market run by R Tracey Heywood assisted by Harry Hopkinson and Ronnie Forsyth. Dairy and Fat Stock were handled on different days. When Poulton held its Agricultural Show there was an enormous influx of beasts, jostling up the ramp from the new Poulton station at the top of the Breck.

Butler's Farm, now gone, was close to Poulton Square and supplied poultry and meat for market days. The tall building was the Slaughter House. Charlie Butler took vegetables round Poulton in a handcart. The whole of this area became the Teanlowe shopping centre.

Besides the milk floats, errand boys and telegram boys, other important 'dashers around the district' were the doctors, who went afar afield as Over-Wyre. William Riddell, known as Dr Bill, started with a horse-drawn carriage, immaculately liveried down to his leather gaiters. The combustion engine had arrived. George Charnley ran Central Garage on Ball Street, but George Dalton, saddler, still had plenty of horses to fit out and the blacksmiths kept going.

But what of the shops that bustling Teanlowe has replaced? Most important were the bakers for 'the staff of life' (with plenty of best butter) was in high regard. The first bread shop on the Breck was Etherington's near the station with Darlington's not far away. Between the two was a tiny-windowed shop where a little black-shawled lady sold all kinds of tripe. The McMullens had their bakery in Station Road, Nicholas delivering on his bicycle fitted with deep basket and snowy, damask cover. There was also Tom Huddlestone's which became the Stocks Cafe. Savoured as much as the freshly baked bread were the hand-raised pork pies from Mayor's, butchers in Market Square – yet another family business.

Among reliable tradesmen, W.H. Bunce was a builder and contractor, J. Foster a qualified chemist (established 1897) who sold wines: Hall's, Vibrona, Wincarnis and Panopepton. Decorator and sign writer James Lincoln was at 40 Tithebarn Street. The Poulton Laundry in Queen's Square asked: 'Is washing at home worth while? Finish washday drudgery, two shillings per dozen articles.' Bailey and Dunkerley owned impressive electric saw mills in Chapel Street while Richards were indispensable for tools, hardware and agricultural necessities. Ainsworth's, who ran Ye Olde Original Toffee Shop, also sold fresh fruit and vegetables.

Poulton was the hub for miles around. To these and other shops can be added hawkers with hand carts piled with fruit, vegetables, rabbits for the cooking pot and freshly caught shrimps from the shore. Tradesmen helped with carts and drays whenever Poulton Gala came round. Their well-groomed horses bedecked in shining brasses and colourful rosettes were a processional asset. Figuring also in this Poulton life before Teanlowe, imagine a jam factory, a glass works, a brick works and a brewery!

Among old Poultonians who welcomed in the twentieth century was Robert Parkinson, descended from the firm of Parkinson and Tomlinson Ltd, corn millers. (Yes, there used to be a corn mill.) He ran a successful grocery business in Queen's Square. When Robert was married in 1884 a red carpet stretched all the way from St Chad's Parish Church to the King's Arms, home of the bride-to-be, Miss Sumner. Before Teanlowe Centre arrived on the scene the inns were very important, but theirs is another story.

When farms disappeared and their marl pits were displaced by the use of fertiliser, market days degenerated into displays of old clothes, pots, tools and knick-knacks the zest and variety of the 1900s markets disappeared. Glorious excitement departed.

CHAPTER FIVE

The Spirit of Christmas Past

'A fair bumping Christmas' was what Fleetwood looked forward to in 1900 and in the years that followed; a time in which every season brought its clear-cut round of activities.

> Christmas broached the merriest ale,
> Christmas told the merriest tale,
> A Christmas gambol oft would cheer,
> A poor man's heart through half the year.

So sang the Victorians one hundred years ago.

A Christmas greetings postcard, dating from 1910. The idea for this kind of thing was made popular in Britain by Prince Albert, Consort of Queen Victoria.

Three Lancashire ladies who made frumenty. On the far right is Ellen Abraham, mother or four fishermen sons, c. 1870. Frumenty, made from cracked wheat, was traditional and sold at fairs and harvest festivals for centuries, only dying out at the end of the twentieth century. Some families served it at breakfast on Christmas Day to stave off hunger until the feast with Christmas goose in the afternoon.

On Wednesday 23 December forty premises advertised in the *Fleetwood Express*, which covered a wide area of Lancashire's Fylde. 'Christmas 1896,' they cried from the shops, some of which were established in the 1830s. Wednesday 24 December was 'Christmas Show Night' when the food shops vied with each other to make the mouth water. If there were vegetarians in those days the slaughter of beasts and fowl must have made them blench. Fish, geese, turkeys, ducks, rabbits, hares and every other kind of game crammed the windows at E. Hall's, Market Street, Blackpool, the most up-to-date premises in the town, but Leadbetter's of North Albert Street, Fleetwood, was acknowledged winner of the 'splendid show' with salmon, live lobsters, 300 turkeys, 50 geese, 120 chickens, pheasants and rabbits from Haverfordwest, hares – and in addition 'a large supply of venison'. Circuit Judge Parry had a big house in Poulton-le-Fylde, but shopped there. B. Leadbetter's slogan in those days when grapes arrived in barrels of cork was 'No foreign produce sold here'.

Philip Williams of West Street specialised in a show of pork. Twenty-four scrubbed pigs were laid out on his marble slab, each with an orange in its mouth, and several other 'porklings' by noted feeders. It was important by whom and how the beasts had been raised and fattened for the great annual feast. From all the farms in the Fylde they came – Larbreck, Lower Grange, Poulton, Gregson's Cartmell's, Mr Bradshaw's of Bispham. W. Jemson's of Holme Farm Carleton. But there was no need for the poor to have scrag-end at Christmas for finest quality mutton fed by T. Baxter of Shard Bridge was only sevenpence halfpenny a pound, not to mention the visits of local Lady Bountifuls who called at 'two up and two down' cottages with extra comforts.

Miss Mary Rimmer of Piper's Penny Bazaar and her staff of six girls were busy at Christmas selling trinkets at a penny a time – one of the Victorian shops on Dock Street, Fleetwood, ablaze with gaslight by 1901. You could

A Christmas card sent on 22 December 1905 to Mrs Jackson of May Villas in Poulton. A simple address then. The villas are still there, situated on what was then called Sheaf Street.

even buy a hat for a penny in those days. Fruiterers and florists advertised foreign fruits, holly, mistletoe 'kissing bushes', chaplets, harps wreaths, hampers of fruit and horticultural sundries. 'Christmas, Christmas, Christmas,' clarioned Nicholas Parkinson of Market Square, with a grand line in bon bons, helmets from 1s 3d, tambourines from 1s, sweets, jewels, games, crackers, figs par excellence, sultanas, muscatels (a box of clusters was 1s). Unfermented wine at 9d a bottle could wash down the apples, nuts, almonds, candied lemon, bacon, hams and gorgonzola cheese. For the truly thirsty the Anglo-Bavarian Brewery Company's Ales arrived in four and a half gallon casks and the festive Season at Yates' Wine Lodge featured hampers of rum, whiskey, good old port, sherry, champagne and brandy. The contents of a guinea hamper appeared enough to keep anyone merry until the next Christmas and included a pound of tea to sober up on. They even gave a shilling back on the empty hamper and bottles.

Children on the alert for the arrival of Santa caught sight of a floating pennant emblazoned 'See the window at Smyth's Bazaars' where there were dolls, magic lanterns and thousands of toys to choose from. Marshall's, next door to the Winter Gardens, Blackpool, already established fifty years, printed a fascinating column which read like a poem: 100 bonbon cosquinques, new designs of dolls with rattles, dolls' houses,

Trips to the Co-op Emporium to see Father Christmas were obligatory for my children Stella, Paul and John. Here they all are in 1959. We were all very sad when the Emporium was pulled down.

An advertisement for the Winter Gardens at Blackpool, 1916.

An advertisement for Goodson's of Deansgate and Oldham Street, Manchester.

swings, Japanese curios, mandolins, buglers, comical mirrors causing broad grins, moving elephants, tail-less donkeys, an endless variety of party games, chocolate goats with carriages. Swiss cottages, toy sofas, tram horses in trams filled with sweets, working toys, clocks with automatic moving fingers, tenders and carriages. It was a display super-abundant, dazzling; while making up your mind you could see the 'Wonderful Lion, the most natural mechanical figure'.

How about hand-painted goods? Screens, plaques, opals, silver-mounted walking-sticks, ivory-backed brushes with silver monograms, silk ties, mufflers, Japanese draught screens, jardinieres, bamboo tables, canterburys, whatnots and wicker chairs. For the ladies – velvets, madras muslins, wool wraps, fichus, embroidered gauze handkerchiefs, heavy chenille portieres, laces, serges and flannels, travelling rugs, furs.

''Tis Christmas. May old and young be merry – our greetings to all; the present season's stock and variety far exceeds any previous effort.' This from the Paragon, leading the van. Seemingly, every Christmas surpassed the one before. There was a great turn-out from Fleetwood to Her Majesty's Opera House, adjoining the Winter Gardens, 'the most comfortable and elegant theatre in Great Britain'. Here was presented the Christmas

A nativity play at Lostock Hall School, Avondale Drive. Here are Miss Smith's pupils in 1958.

pantomime Little Bo Beep on Boxing Day with magnificent scenery and costumes.

The part of Bo Peep was played by Dorothy Vernon, then one of England's reigning great beauties. This was coupled with a grand speciality Carnival culminating in the inevitable Transformation Scene, 'The Child's Christmas Dream of Joy', featuring the traditional appearance of Harlequin, Columbine and Pantaloon, Stalls and dress circle *2s 6d*, gallery *6d* and special late trains laid on to all parts. Imagine Christmas 1896 giving a performance of Handel's *Messiah* with four principals and chorus of 150, plus band – all for sixpence in old money. There was carol singing in Albert Square; brass bands were blaring, church bells chiming, errand boys with over-loaded delivery bikes making last-minute dashes to the homes of the gentry. The Victorians thought of everything, even the antidote – Cockle's anti–bilious pills – never known to fail.

We still found Christmas to be a time of magic down all the years when we were growing up in the twentieth century. However, looking back to the Victorian ideal it appears that even in our childhood days things scarcely

Wide-eyed at Christmas! Our first-born, Catherine Stella, in 1952.

compared. Since then it has further gone downhill, the magic swallowed by commercialism. What would the average child say now if he or she awoke to one stocking containing one sugar pig, an orange, a few nuts and a net (a small net) of chocolate coins covered with silver paper?

CHAPTER SIX

Tar Boilers, Shops & Whitsuntide

As little tots, my brothers and I, when so inclined, constructed tents. There were two kinds we made: the summer type for out of doors used a rectangle of hessian sacking, whose longer side was placed horizontally on a brick wall, and nailed there along the top edge at a convenient height. Two broomstales (sticks), various lengths of string, and several tent pegs judiciously placed formed a canopy under which we conducted our palavers. The winter tent consisted of two discarded full-length curtains, which were draped over a square dining table in the manner of a large tablecloth, the ends reaching the floor. Helping in the winter camping game (we took our own refreshments in summer), Mother conveniently laid two freshly buttered currant teacakes on a plate before the flap entrance for us to eat inside. To increase realism, for we were romantically inclined, we made a nodding acquaintance with the inclement weather outside, especially when it was very squally, and would temporarily quit our tent and hide between the heavy draught curtain and the outside kitchen door. For some reason this had to be done on hands and knees, standing was not permitted, and with the door slightly ajar we would peer round, inhaling deeply of the cold air, shivering in happy anticipation at the hardships without and the warmth and friendliness within.

Later tents were not essential: we would invent, pretend and dramatise whenever the need arose as all children do, if the materials were not to hand: it was often enough, if the grass was plentiful and dry in summer to lie there and dream . . .

> *Ich ruhe still im hohen grunen Gras*
> I rest quietly in the tall green grass
> *Und sende lange meinen Blick nach oben,*
> And steadily look upwards,
> *Von Grillen rings umschwirrt ohn Unterlass,*
> Crickets ceaselessly stridulate around me,
> *Von Himmelsblaue wundersam umwoben.*
> And I am surrounded by a sky of blue.

Die schonen weissen Wolken zeihn dahin
The lovely drifting white clouds
Durchs tiefe Blau, wie schone stille Traume; . . .
Sail through the deep blue like beautiful quiet dreams; . . .

So wrote Hermann Allmers in his 'Feldeinsamkeit', 'Solitude in Summer Fields'. To lie lazily and watch the slow purposeful, silent procession of cumulus clouds was sufficient pleasure in itself.

Like most children I became excited when I 'discovered' things that took my fancy, stimulated my imagination or stirred my sense of beauty. In themselves these things could be quite simple and might not have moved many children as they did me: a few mossy steps, seemingly coming from nowhere and projecting from an overgrown bank; an ancient gnarled tree of interesting shape; an uncommon fungus, especially if it had a highly coloured cap. A spring of water, cold and clear, rising from the earth and flowing through the forest of sphagnum bog moss to join the nearest stream down the hill would give me great delight.

It was Mother who started us off and her vital and infectious curiosity in life made all learning pleasure, reading, writing and arithmetic included. Mother gave freely of her time; even during housework or shopping there was opportunity to draw our attention to something. She told us of the

The opening of Oswaldtwistle tram car service. Alderman Mrs Lawson is seen here driving one of the first tram cars in the early years of the twentieth century. A large crowd had assembled for what was a major event at the time.

Yeoman of the Guard pictured on the packet of Gossage's Lifeguard Soap on washday, and explained why the good ship *Unity*, a vessel of the Manchester Co-operative Society merchant fleet, should be sailing across a three pound packet of Federation self-raising flour every Wednesday baking day. She called us to listen to the sounds around us: the song of the lark in Farmer Hardy's fields; the call of lapwing and the wind thrumming through the telephone wires as we walked up Hodges Lane; the hissing of the wind passing through yellowing, dried grasses on the steep bank of the reservoir. She pointed out ladies' smocks in the ditch and the heart shape of the lime leaves overhead with the sweet smelling of its flowers in July. One day, as we sat on a felled beech trunk eating a picnic tea after school she pointed to the vast bulk of the dirigible R34 airship, passing high above us like a great silver sausage with the RAF red, white and blue roundel on her hull.

There was the interest in watching people perform their daily tasks in the community: bricklayers, road maintenance men, painters and the like. 'Mr Pinner', our name for the gentleman from the water board who visited the village streets every quarter and flushed the mains, was almost as commonplace as the policeman or lamplighter, and we took little notice as he passed by. On the way to school we might see someone not too common like a surveyor or a gang felling a dangerous tree, but when I attended a secondary school five miles away, by train, the chances of seeing something fresh greatly increased. For instance, at the station we travelled to was a large timber yard and I counted myself lucky when the man with the adze was working. With this heavy cutting tool wielded by the right arm in a chopping motion he 'tooled down' the greater irregularities in tree trunks used for callender bowls (rollers used in textile and paper manufacture), and later to finer limits to be machined on a lathe. In his initial attack great chips of wood flew heavily around him but later, when the bowl seemed sufficiently cylindrical and finished, he would still draw off long shavings. What a keen eye for symmetry he had and a sure, practised hand! I put this artisan in a similar class to that of the famous medieval painter who drew a perfect circle with one flourish of the wrist as a practical example of his skill.

Whooping cough, which many children caught in winter at the most inconvenient times, could be alleviated, old wives said, by walking twice round the gasworks. Equally efficacious was to linger in the vicinity of roads works where a tar boiler was in use. The ailment is still with us but the remedies have disappeared, probably for good. Gas is now produced cleanly from the North Sea and there is no longer the falling rain of black grit, nor the intermittent belching of nigrescent smoke and hazy red flame from the horizontal retorts. One can no longer watch the busy saddle tank engines pulling loaded coal trucks nor indulge to the full in the stench of coal gas that clung everlastingly to the areas around gasworks. Whether the smoke, soot fall-out or smell of coal-tar acids now produced in the National Coal Board patent fuels plants (under the Clean Air Act – clean, that is, for all but the unfortunate persons living thereabouts) are as effective for pulmonary complaints, we shall perhaps never know.

The tar boiler, always seen sooner or later at every street excavation or road maintenance, was a lumbering wheeled tank of large dimensions. It was provided with a tall chimney stack at one end and a firebox at the other other, and was reminiscent of nothing so much as a small and simplified Puffing Billy stripped of its cranks and driving levers. A foot beneath the chimney projection was a huge tap from which the hot, melted tar flowed into the pails, scoops and other utensils used to carry the glistening jet black liquid. Where stone setts were the basic road material the tar, used as an amalgam, was poured into the interstices between the stones already half-filled with roadstone chippings. In later days tar coated the concrete surface of the road and used as an adhesive, held the stone chippings, in graded layers, scattered thereon.

Gas works and road works were most useful as diversions and helped to take the mind off wearying school matters. There were also other things that helped one to dilly-dally on the way.

There were three types of steam road engine that one might possibly, nay, one *hoped* to meet on the road. First, the showman's engine with a curved canopy supported on four polished brass, barley twist pillars and, placed before the chimney, having a dynamo running by belt and pulley from the

A heavy road roller kept behind Richards' Ironmongers. This was the oldest business in Fylde. Rollers like this one would have been used to lay roads like the East Lancashire Road in the 1920s.

Traction engines like this one, seen at a steam rally, would have been used for roadmaking and for threshing at harvest time.

flywheel. The brothers and I remember watching for some considerable time, until we had to return home at sunset, while a gang struggled to save one of these engines from sinking for ever beneath the corner of a notorious swampy field. We assumed they saved it but later, two unfortunate house buyers were to bless their misfortune when later still they purchased the same patch of land, this time with a pair of semi-detached houses on it. The houses, like those built on sand that Jesus spoke of, fell.

The steam roller resembled the showman's engine but in a more utilitarian way, and had large spoked wheels at the rear as had the showman's engine, but whereas the roller had a large roller on which one end of the boiler rested the other engine had a pair of wheels at the front. The third member of the trio was the haulage engine. It was smaller than its relations, had a vertical, smaller boiler, could raise steam more quickly, carry a greater load and move faster, too. It was used by heavy hauliers carrying flour, timber and the like, on its own wagon. Very occasionally one saw it pulling an extra long and heavy load on a trailer crocodile burdened with a giant boiler or condenser. Of these machines (apart from those carefully demonstrated in exhibitions since) nothing but the memory remains of whirling eccentrics, spinning governors and a smell of hot lubricating oil piercing the thin haze of smoke and exhaust steam and a following of eager, small boys, anxious to be offered, but never quite getting a free ride.

The horse as power for haulage (excepting those that brewers use partly as an advertising ploy) is an obsolete idea. Years ago they were commonplace but always impressive, especially in the combination of tandem, a well-matched pair of shires drawing behind them a large dray of grey cloth or finished paper in enormous rolls four feet or so in diameter, or a high load of esparto grass with its strong smell not at all like sweet country hay. Those horses were so familiar with their routes that they stopped and started without any promptings, and would show impatience at an overlong wait by sharply striking the setts with a right fore shoe.

Desire for change took us from the street to visit other areas of children's activities. I never knew why we went to one place (and only during winter) unless it was to warm our hands against the end house of a terrace where there was a warm area where the kitchen fireback stood. Here we assembled, side by side, with our palms and backs flattened against the brickwork. We never played games there, nor shouted, for quietness was strictly observed; obviously we had discovered that provided we behaved in that fashion we were allowed on sufferance.

There were times when we walked to Willie Frazer's. He was the first man in the village, apart from the two doctors, to own a car. It was a Napier, a six-seater open tourer with wire-spoked wheels and folding canvas hood and having long running boards fitted with aluminium treads. Perhaps there was a space on them for a shrouded spare wheel standing against the car side in a little curved channel something like an egg in an eggcup, if you know what I mean. Willie had the largest newsvendor's shop, and he always wore a tweed knickerbocker suit, with thick, woollen, double topped stockings and brown leather brogues which had a punched pattern on the toecap. He had a fair-sized moustache, curled just like the horns of a water buffalo, and waxed at the tips.

His shop had much treasure. We lined ourselves outside the windows, 'bagging' this or that or the other, but inside excitement mounted as more wonders came into view. Here the most expensive toys and reading books, annuals and fascinating novelties were sold; here the latest boxes of Christmas crackers, here the most ostentatious Christmas decorations and here the most expensive wallets and boxes of stationery – not that we were interested in writing – that was work! Here, too, if one joined the Christmas Club one went with one's parent to choose a book or a toy in the arranged price range. My brothers and I bought our set of Wonder Book annuals here, but one year I decided on a change and chose one quite unlike the usual run of children's books. It had the most fascinating covers in an all-over pattern, blue and white, of rampant gryphons, which I read had been copied from the original pattern in a London museum – the V&A, no less! I recorded the fact though it meant nothing to me then. 'Was I sure,' Willie asked me,' was I really sure that I wanted the book called Number Two Joy Street?' Of course I was sure: the covers alone were exciting and a glimpse of the beautiful wood-engravings within (a form of art I had already learned to appreciate) stirred my imagination quite deeply; goodness only knew what lay within besides!

The authors' names were names and nothing more but I had set my heart on the book and would be unsatisfied until it was in possession, but notice who the authors were and all under one cover. There was *Prince Rabbit* (A.A. Milne); *The Dragon at Hide and Seek* (G.K. Chesterton); *Lucy* (Walter de la Mare); *A Thing to be Explained* (Lawrence Houseman); *The Stranger* (Hugh Walpole); *A Cautionary Tale* by Hilaire Belloc; and so many, many more. Edith Sitwell wrote a poem for it, and Rose Fyleman – 'The Princess of Kensington' and 'They', respectively, if my memory is not at fault after this lapse of sixty years. It opened a new world to me. It was in that book that I first heard of Sussex where so much beauty dwelt. No wonder I grew up to be a librarian!

Of course, that didn't stop me from reading penny comics, though by the time I had the book, comics were no longer staple fare, and Willie sold a whole selection of these: *Jester and Funny Wonder* on Saturday; *Comic Cuts* on Tuesday; *Chips* on Wednesday. Two others which we were not encouraged to read lest they brought disturbed sleep (they had a slightly stronger content) were *Golden Penny* and *Butterfly*. All the characters therein contained, Constable Cuddlecook, Weary Willie and Tired Tim, Sammy and Jackie the Circus Twins, Roland Butter and Hammon Egg, Mustafa Bunn and the Jam Sponge and all the rest, amused us until twopenny magazines took over with *Magnet*, *Popular*, *Wizard*, *Rover*, *Union Jack*, *Sexton Blake and Scout*, *Chums* and *Modern Boy*. They certainly kept us reading, reading – and criticising.

Willie Frazer's was at the end of the village main shopping thoroughfare, Butterthorn Lane where shop design was about equally divided between the purpose-built ones on the south side – not a good side for a shop but they could not choose since the other side had got there long before – and these, the north-facing shops. These latter had begun as private dwellings in the early nineteenth century and had then developed a trade in some commodity or other. It had then been justifiable to extend premises by the addition of a one-storeyed room from the front door, and this was clearly seen in some shops, for as the customer entered, the assistant, summoned by the clanging bell, descended the steps at the rear of the shop from the living quarters via the front entrance of the original house.

The largest shop was at right angles to the lane, a grocery store, the Co-operative Society, in Stores Street. Like all grocers of the time the Co-op did much of their pre-packaging on the premises in clearly distinguishable bags: sugar in blue sugar paper; washing soda in brown ditto; currants, raisins, and sultanas respectively in purple, magenta and yellow kraft paper. Cheese (unless in maker's pack) was sold only in absorbent cheese paper, on which the cheese, if in any way moist, had left bright yellow stains. Biscuits were seldom wrapped and could be viewed before purchase through the window above the square biscuit tin. Education was part of the

Myself (far right) and Joan Marsh, both aged 10, holding a banner in a Whit Walk during a procession down Newtown Street. I lived at no. 39. This is one of Father's postcard photographs.

Co-op self-improvement plan – as it still is, though by no means to the same extent – and our branch, like many another, had a department devoted to this social need. There was an upper room over the shop used as a library on Saturday afternoons, presided over by an elderly librarian, spectacled, and so interested in his books that I fancy he would have preferred to have been left alone to his love. The borrower presented himself at a window where a complete library list was handed out for him to make a choice. He could not browse and examine; there simply wasn't the room for space was at a minimum. This is one reason why this library was in decline; another was that at about this time many newsagents were setting up small libraries of light fiction, Sapper, Edgar Wallace, Sidney Horler, Ethel M. Dell, Jeffery Farnol and the like, where one could borrow at a trifling cost a new book at each visit. The third reason was that a small county branch library was built in the village, but by that time I had left secondary school behind me. As I said there were other educational facilities: concerts and recitals; competitions and musical festivals; rambling and camping clubs and opportunities for economical holidays. All these were valued and put to excellent use. The sponsoring of passive entertainments by many present day firms is not quite the same thing. With the Co-op you *had* to take part if you wished to benefit – as I said before it was self-help in the best tradition.

Butterthorn Lane was a focal point, a place to meet people one had not seen for some time. Annually it was the starting point and terminus of the Whitsun walks, those religious processions held at Pentecost and probably very similar to that one mentioned by Charlotte Brontë in *Shirley*. We did not, like her differing denominations, violently disagree; instead we all, Anglicans and Free Churchmen (our Roman brethren politely withdrew from the scheme), took our turn to lead the united procession of witness on an annual rota of precedence. What a day! What a festival so eagerly awaited for, especially by the young ladies – with their new frocks, and those a little older with their new outfits! What bravely blaring brass bands! What a flaunting of florally festooned texts! What boldly borne banners breasting the breeze, each carried by two men while four young women straining at their two-colour banner cords like guy ropes to a tent, and keeping the billowing material upright, bend their heads and place the palms of their free hands on the crowns of their large, picture hats, in a gallant effort to keep them on! The young damsels, from those newly entered into the kindergarten to those who have reached the middle school, loosely hold white ribbons and carry elegant baskets of fragrant flowers, charming all hearts as they are photographed by older friends again and again. Small boys, with unaccustomed brushed hair, held down by water or a little oil, more smartly dressed than salesmen from one of the more distinguished showrooms and sporting buttonholes of rose or carnation, proudly present themselves to relations and neighbours, collecting pennies in a breast pocket. Fathers in new suits; choir in surplices and servers in cottas of dazzling white, newly starched by the ladies of the church; Scouts, Cubs, Brownies, Guides, Rovers and Rangers – all in neat uniforms; clergy in stocks and stoles and dog collars with prayers of thanks said silently for the warm, sunny weather all gathered in Butterhorn Lane to testify by their presence that Christian unity, if not here and now, was definitely on its way. Almost to the end of the second decade of the century each separate denomination returned to its own schoolroom after the procession to take afternoon tea, although, if the weather was really warm and no rain had fallen for some time, the Congregationalists took over a field for the afternoon and had a picnic tea. By the beginning of the thirties the preparation for this chore, which largely devolved on the ladies, especially the matrons, seemed to have become more than a little irksome. Serving tea to many children can be a hazard for new clothes so it was therefore abandoned by general assent. In any case tea parties were no longer considered a treat; even the long-established Tea Garden, which had been popular with the lower middle and artisan classes for the whole of the previous century, was now in rapid decline.

We measured the year by the greater festivals of the Church and these were brought before us by the by-products of special fairings, perhaps not the ideal way, but it had a soundness in practice. Modern youth still partakes of some of these: Christmas with presents, Shrove Tuesday with pancakes and Easter with pace and chocolate eggs. We also observed Mid Lent or Refreshment or Mothering Sunday with little bunches of flowers for Mother and Simnel cake for the rest of the household. Then there were Palm Sunday (palm crosses) and Good Friday (hot cross buns). Some areas had extra celebrations, such as Fig Pie Sunday (Blackburn), Blackcurrant Sunday (Heywood) and the presentation of God cakes, triangular pastries filled with a spiced mincemeat filling, in the town of Bolton. Every church and chapel had its 'Sermons' or Anniversary Sunday. We also remembered Ascension Day when the older children of the village school after attending church and morning day school went on a picnic in a charabanc to a local beauty spot and picnic area.

A short distance from Butterhorn Lane was Big Croft. We generally avoided it for children there greatly outnumbered our gang from Little Back and in the croft we were regarded as trespassers and petty rivals. Here was other interest, though, in the being of Bert Fisher and his charabanc. To the ignorant the charabanc was nothing more than a perambulating clutch

The 2nd East Lancashire Regiment Lytham Volunteer Band photographed outside Lytham Hall in about 1900.

A group of Lancashire Methodists in a White Rose Motors charabanc in about 1927.
A distant cousin, Jessie Howarth, is at the front of the vehicle, holding the baby.

of church pews, if you can imagine that, and the precursor of the motor coach, every pew or bank a long, upholstered bench seat stretching the width of the vehicle. There was no central aisle running the length of the chassis; instead one entered by a half door on the near side. Every bench seat had its own half door – and there must have been up to six on each side in a larger charabanc, though these were smaller vehicles with only half that number and less than half the capacity. With folded canvas hood there were no side screens: we bowled along the quiet lanes with a responsible child seated against each door with its upright trigger or polished brass handle, as happy as happy could be, singing a song we had learned in school or a song of the moment heard in a seaside music hall. The pace was leisurely and limited to twelve miles per hour, certainly not suitable for a motorway!

CHAPTER SEVEN

The Price of Fame

In the early years of the twentieth century when the population of Lytham was 2,000 and the Italian giant boxer Primo Carnera scored his first knock-out at Madison Square Garden beating Big Boy Peterson in less than half a round, Lytham had grown to realise they had a knock-out celebrity too – an artist of fame.

The site of the old lighthouse at Ansdell, which fell down. The Ribble estuary is in the background.

Walls made from pebbles from the shore: the kind that surrounded Richard Ansdell's house, Starr Hills. Staining Windmill can be seen in the background.

Richard Ansdell RA, nature and animal painter, had decided to build a house among the marram grass-clad sand hills and to call it Starr Hills. Starr grass was another name for the wiry, grey-green grass which held the sand dunes together. As far back as the Middle Ages there was a Keeper of the Lord's Starr Grass. He made sure that no one removed it for thatching cottages!

Stretching towards Blackpool were several miles of these sandhills. It was a wild, lonely spot that appealed to the artist, but his friends thought him crazy to settle there, so far away from London. However, some fellow artists joined him later. Thomas Webster commissioned The Elms and there followed Edenfield and Fairlawn, houses of character. Cobble stones from the shore made picturesque boundary walls.

The boy who was to become so famous that he gave his name to a district and a railway station was born in the stirring year of 1815. His talent first showed as a Blue Coat charity boy in Liverpool where he submitted two pictures to the Royal Academy, London. 'Dead Game' was awarded a prize of £10.

One of his paintings, 'The Herd Lassie', was presented by John Booth of Barton Hall, Preston, related to Dr Booth who for thirty years was Medical

Patrick stands beside an old abandoned anchor on St Annes beach, with the 'lonely sea and sky' in the background. Beyond is the River Ribble.

Officer of Health for St Annes. Ansdell's 'The ploughing match' is owned by the Tate Gallery in London.

By 1853 the artist was exhibiting local scenes, for the solitariness, the great expanse of sky inspired him. His painting of 'Lytham Common' remains of special interest for it was the site upon which St Annes-on-Sea was built. On the Common was then a tiny hamlet called Heyhouses.

Starr Hills was finished and lived in by 1860. Press notices were flying up and down the country. Alys Myers of *The North Countryman* wrote, '. . . Corridors and rooms hung with pictures. A Picture Gallery? But no! This is Lytham St Annes Town Hall where even the Council Chamber has its share of oil paintings in ornate gilt frames. The pictures are by Victorian artist Richard Ansdell who has given his name to a district and to a railway station as well.'

What was Lytham like when Richard Ansdell was in residence? By the 1830s the population had risen to 1,523 and the resort was so popular that Lytham's ancient church could not accommodate all worshippers. Bathing vans were also inadequate (although some visitors went to church in them on wet Sundays). The *Daily Telegraph* reported that the esplanade and the firm sands left by receding tide were alive with people.

*Lytham Windmill, photographed in
2002. It now houses a museum in
the basement and has had new
sails fitted by the Gillett brothers,
local craftsmen.*

A branch line was opened connecting the resort with Preston and Wyre Railway. The first train rumbled in with dignitaries on 16 February 1846 to the sound of cheers and the firing of a cannon. 1863 brought the railway line to Blackpool. A road was built along the boundary of Richard's land and where the railway crossed the road was Ansdell Halt. The famous artist was not well pleased.

The artist became president of Liverpool Academy, won gold medals and was considered to be better than the famous Landseer. He exhibited 180 paintings in London alone selling at an average price of £750 each. Steel engravings of his originals hung in every Victorian drawing room but it had proved one thing to plan solitude, another to keep it.

The building of the town of St Annes was slow in early years because of the short terms on which land leases were granted. This retarded growth but when the period was extended to 60, 90 and 999 years this was encouraging and promoted prosperity.

As for Starr Hills, it was later the residence of Major Hincksman and was also used as a hospital for war wounded. Richard Ansdell died in 1885, an early example of the price of fame being the loss of one's privacy. Today's merciless media coverage throws up examples week after week.

In the carefree days of childhood, climbing sandhills was our delight, gathering evening primrose and sighting tiny lizards among the pale green starr grass. Because of blowing sand, as Lytham St Annes grew I remember

St Cuthbert's Church, Lytham, in the late nineteenth century.

in later years a decision was made to move the dunes, but to us children this took away most of the mystery and magic with which our early adventures had been invested.

As for Mother, she shared spiritual calm with Richard Ansdell, prizing the tranquillity and preferring the lonely land and seascapes of St Annes to the noisy brashness of jolly Blackpool.

CHAPTER EIGHT

Sweet Charity

O n a Sunday and Monday of long ago, of four centuries past, at the waning of the moon and the very height of spring tides, a violent tempest of wind swept the north-west seas inland, deluging corn, destroying cottages, washing down sea fences and in general creating watery havoc. The only buildings of any size in the Lytham area of 1720 were Clifton Hall and the Vicarage. The rest, about forty dwellings plus barns of hay, suffered so badly that Robert Bawbell and the others presented a humble petition asking for a brief to request charitably disposed persons to contribute towards redressing this act of God.

Butterflies and flowers arriving at Lower Green (the site of an ancient village green) in 1937.

They hoped for £2,055 to repair damage but received only £103. They got together to decide how to spend it, adding other charitable gifts – five pounds from the Revd William Threlfall and three guineas from Mr Elston of Commonside. It needed a miracle like the five barley loaves and two small fishes that fed the five thousand to make all possible.

Wisely they put the sum, in its entirety, towards creating a free school. Wise indeed, for the land in which they invested became the centre of Blackpool and the Talbot Road area. The success of Robert Bawbell and friends is still one to marvel at for two centuries later, added to by William Gaulter and John Harrison, the charity was worth £333,000.

Charity abounded, too, in the Club Days and galas traditional in June, the month of roses. Everyone enjoyed themselves and the holding of galas spread to all corners of the old Fylde of Lancashire.

Poulton-le-Fylde successfully re-instated theirs in the early 1960s but some villages can claim an unbroken run apart from omission during the war years. Lytham, Singleton, Thornton, Kirkham and Carleton were typical of small townships holding this particular event-packed summer spree, anticipated as eagerly as Christmas.

Passed down from Club Days, which consisted of a simple procession beautified by silk banners from the Lodges and Working Men's Institutes, because these were so enjoyed, like Topsy the processions grew. Galas

Queen Kathleen Wilkinson with train bearers Jimmy Gleeson and Peter Robinson, c. 1939. The crown bearer was Gerald Winder.

The Red Rose Band in the 2005 Poulton Gala parade.

St John's May Queen, Monica Bennett, c. 1938.

On very special occasions such as galas and coronations, it was traditional to roast an ox and the whole village would line up, each with a plate for slices. This one is for Clitheroe in 1911. Fleetwood had one in the same year. The professional ox-roasters came from Clitheroe.

included crowning the Rose Queen by a local celebrity, sports such as sack, wheelbarrow, foot, egg and spoon races with a little fair thrown in and tasty eats and drinks, home made for good measure, rounded off events.

Village vied with village. It was every girl's dream to ride in a landau amid her retinue and be crowned Rose Queen. A great feature was the skilled dancing of Morris groups who practised assiduously and took part not merely in their own gala but in neighbouring ones. The skills were passed down by charitably minded people, 'Daddy Glass' of Fleetwood and Billy Livesey, keen Morris dancer who, as a boy, was one of Carleton's troupe. He grew up to train the dancers himself and advise on the intricacies of Maypole dancing (the village butcher stored the maypole.) Distinctive in dress, Carleton's troupe wore white, decked with bright green sashes. They assembled outside the village school at Town End on a Wednesday in June led by Poulton's brass band, the latter, founded on 25 September 1875, being an indispensable, charitable organisation! The gala procession would move to Pye's at Carleton Lodge or to Norcross where they gave a performance of Morris dancing, thoroughly deserving of the cakes, biscuits and home-made lemonade that followed. Billy was a tailor so costumes were also good. The ladies sat up all night to make paper roses for decorating floats, harness and the graceful, wrought-iron arch at Castle Gardens Inn, now long since gone.

Perhaps the money raised was small but the goodwill and participation went far beyond Lotto! It was, indeed, sweet charity.

CHAPTER NINE

Smithereens

Although I admire crystal, all those beautiful cut-glass tumblers and silver-bound rose bowls coruscating with rainbow colours or sparkling in the sunshine like diamonds, I never buy them. The reason is I fear we would not be together for long. I have a horror of smashing glass or in any way witnessing its breakage.

There cannot be another to equal my hat trick, that is, to break a pane of glass, by accident, on each of three successive birthdays. On these shattering days I lost most of my birthday gift money, for none was a small pane and twenty ounce glass was never cheap. The recipient of one of my unfortunate missiles demanded of my father thirty-two ounce glass for that ruinous erection he had the impertinence to call a greenhouse. It fell down with the next strong wind, after my glass had been replaced. I hugged myself with unholy glee, but there seems to be a distinct possibility that the damage I inflicted on the glass rebounded to act traumatically on my subconscious for, since those days of misfortune, I have been ever aware of the potential short life of glass when wrongly handled.

There was no doubt at all; the weather was heading for a violent storm from the hills. Deeper and deeper grew the gloom although it was yet early afternoon. The hills stood in slate-blue outline against a dark grey sky. There was a grim silence, although lightning was flickering on the horizon, and the rain kept off. The undulating moan of rising wind began, quite subdued at first like the wind through a keyhole and, as pressure fell, the shriller sound of sharp-edged eaves joined the chorus, plus the woofing bellow of a long, narrow corridor. Then, without warning, a span of steel sheeting, part of an old Anderson shelter, lifted into the air from a builder's yard nearby and was thrown into a field alongside. The school greenhouse, Dutch pattern glass-to-ground design, with its clips instead of old-fashioned putty, stood no chance in the heavy gusts and panes were flicked out of their places one by one, like a magician flicking cards on the stage, and were dashed hither and thither as the winds directed.

The boys had already begun their singing lesson with my brother in the Hall, a high and large room with windows whose size was considerable, the centre pane of each being about eight feet square. The choice the boys had made was 'Onward Christian Soldiers' and they started with vigour. Funnily enough, when the rousing chorus began, the air vacuum outside

It was at a family house near this farm at Clitheroe that the mystery of the glass tumbler occurred which led to a family outing being spoiled, but which had a funny side. Our family outings were all enjoyable apart from one which had to be abandoned. A drunken driver crashed into a lamp standard in front of our house at 2 o'clock in the morning.

became too much for the middle pane nearest to us and, with a soughing crash, it was sucked out of its setting and showered onto the garden. Such is the astonishing reaction of youth that immediately the boys cried out, 'Let's have another verse and do another window.'

At one time in the possession of my family were two portions of a broken wine glass. They were of thickened glass, rather crude stuff I felt, and had a thick stem and heavy foot. I wondered why the pieces had been saved when it was obvious that they were useless for holding any kind of liquid.

Several decades before I made my appearance in this world my father's family were up betimes one bright summer morning preparing for their annual visit to the seaside. With ample time and plans seemingly well-ordered there was no need to hurry, but during this carefree period there was an unusual disturbance as a result of which all the timing came to naught and certain members of the party were most upset. The morning was still and cool, and the house was airy as it stood near the hills.

As a family we could all share in the joys of trainspotting. We watched Mallard *steam through Poulton and met Alan Pegler driving the* Royal Scot. *Railway relics were a special interest. This is a crowd of trainspotters at Bury.*

Suddenly, from the direction of the room still lying in shadow came a loud crack like a rifle being fired. There was no person in the room and nothing seemed to have been disturbed. However, the superstitious members of the household demanded a thorough search before packing another holiday item. At length it was noticed that an old goblet kept in an oak, glass-fronted display cabinet had broken into two pieces. It stood isolated; nothing had fallen on it nor had it fallen itself since the foot stood firm, but a circular crack had appeared, beginning at the bowl and turning one and a half perimeters before finishing at the lip. Alas, the feeling of something that could not be readily explained settled upon the party. Things began to go wrong; tempers became frayed; the children turned awkward, and the time schedule fell apart. When at last the cab arrived, collected and delivered the party at the railway station, the train had already left, and all bewailed the fact. Later, however, the adults pondered when they learned that the train they had missed had crashed and several passengers had lost their lives.

Now the really odd thing about this story is that although I've seen that broken object, handled it and can find no reason for its breakage, I recall that I have heard the same or a similar story from other parts of this country. That is the mystery.

The dining room walls were of hard plaster and the lofty room had clerestories; the floor was parquet and the pillars of concrete-sheathed steel girders. To cut down resonance, a heavy velvet curtain had been draped along two walls but there was still an aggressive echo that became painful to the ear when sound rose above a certain decibel level. As one has probably guessed, the room was in a boys' school. At lunchtime, full of noisy, hungry boys anxious to be eating, the clatter became too much for comfort. In lesson time this room doubled as a music room; indeed the architect had designed it for that purpose, so the Head of Department (my brother Charles) was considered to be a fit and proper person to take charge as often as possible since he was already proofed against ear damage.

It thus fell to my brother's lot to move from table to table, admonishing the nearest boy whose voice rose above the level of normal conversation or reminding another that his left-hand eating tool was not a tuning fork. At one formica-topped table a junior boy was filling eight tumblers with water from a jug. Charles watched idly as the water in the fifth tumbler rose above the halfway mark. Suddenly there were only seven tumblers and the boy was pouring a steady stream of water onto the table. Realising that the fifth tumbler had disappeared, he gave a short cry and stopped pouring. With his mouth wide open, staring at the spot where the missing tumbler had stood, he looked at Charles and said, 'It's gone!'

'Yes,' Charles agreed, but where had it gone? There seemed to be no trace of its passing. By now the rest of the occupants of the table were fully absorbed by the mystery but no one asked a question; they just stared at each other. All this time, the unheeded water dripped on the floor and around the usual uproar of noise continued as if nothing out of the ordinary had happened. At that particular moment one of the boys opposite the water pourer did something which I have wondered about for years. He passed his right hand through his thick, springy hair and a shower of glass fragments like a handful of sugar crystals flowed out of his locks and onto the table. I have since discovered that soprano singers hitting high operatic notes can achieve the same result on glass!

Did you know that broken glass before recycling is called cullet? The word is derived from the Latin 'collum', meaning neck, from that lazy habit mentioned by Poe in his 'Cask of Amontillado' of breaking off the neck of the wine bottle rather than withdrawing the cork. There must have been a superabundance of broken glass after a wild party in those days!

CHAPTER TEN

Polly & Dolly

Will you still be remembered as in 'institution' or 'character' a century after your passing? Such can be said of an Over-Wyre girl born in 1811 to John and Margaret Hodgkinson. Christened Dorothy, she soon became known to all as Dolly and eventually 'Old Doilee'. She married Richard Riley, a Fleetwood pilot, and they settled in a Knott End cottage which was old even then, bearing the date 1713. Their first child, Thomas, was only fifteen months old when one stormy night Richard was swept overboard to his death. The widow set up a tea shop in her white, low-eaved cottage in order to make ends meet.

Dolly's Cottage, Knott End, 1890.

The Bourne Arms Inn at Knott End, 1910. It was a haven from shipwrecked sailors like those on the Utility.

Dolly made a good job of bringing up Thomas, who became apprenticed to a builder. A hard worker and intelligent, in early manhood Thomas opened his own joiner's shop behind his mother's cottage and from such small beginnings built up a highly successful firm in Fleetwood. His ironmonger's shop in North Albert Street, situated on the corner opposite the present library, had magnificent mahogany woodwork in its interior, in particular a fine carved staircase.

In 1850 Thomas founded the North Lancashire Steam Saw Mills in Fleetwood; he also built Wyre View Terrace, adjoining Dolly's Cottage. At that time attempts were afoot to turn Knott End into a posh seaside resort. A new name, St Bernard's-On-Sea, was dreamed up but it never caught on. Besides house-building in Fairhaven, contracts for Fairhaven Lake, part of Blackpool Sea Wall and construction work for the Lancashire and Yorkshire Railway all came his way. His friend Samuel Laycock, the Lancashire dialect poet, wrote verses in praise of Thomas's success. No doubt they met when Samuel was for a time in charge of the Whitworth institute in Dock Street. Meanwhile, Dolly, the sweet stay-at-home, well content, was attracting her own brand of fame. Visitors came in their scores to the quaint fishing cottage and took back tales of Dolly's scones and strawberry jam to all parts of Lancashire and Yorkshire. Dolly's Cottage was a landmark in the centre of Knott End, not only for its thatched roof (eventually replaced by a corrugated iron roof) but for the large cage which hung in the porch. This contained a talking parrot which had belonged to a sailor who perhaps

These ladies were Knott End village washerwomen in the days of communal mangles and ovens.

parted with it for one of Old Doilee's mouth-watering teas. That we don't know, but what has passed down as gospel truth is that the bird, after years of nautical company, 'swore like billy ho', thus providing entertainment for passers-by and scoffers of scones.

When the *People's Magazine* came to interview Dolly in 1904 she had become something of a legend. She was then Mrs Carter, having become the wife of James Carter, also a Fleetwood pilot. The magazine found her, aged 93, 'full of health and vigour and looking like Queen Victoria in a snow-white apron'. Unlike Queen Victoria, however, it is on record that she greeted reporters in rich Over-Wyre dialect: 'Come on in, all on ye. Sit yer down and mak yersells a whoam.'

She outlived her second husband and her son, who at his death left a vast establishment and a prosperous business. The Riley Ward at Fleetwood Hospital was established in his memory. But it is Dolly who is still remembered. The cottage has gone, the old fishing ways vanished, but to this day, if you ask in Over-Wyre someone will be able to tell you where Dolly's Cottage used to stand. I have often wondered what happened to the parrot. Polly and Dolly were at one time inseparable and both quietly famous in their own way. However, I have it on good authority Polly was anything but quiet!

CHAPTER ELEVEN

Bewitching Pendle

Because my paternal grandmother was born at Downham, visits to Clitheroe and the Ribble Valley were part of the family scene for years. The stirring history of Pendle Hill itself, steeped in witchcraft stories, even four centuries after the drama was played out, came home to me early in my young life. The wildness of those moors and the pageants held at Clitheroe were spell-binding. A grim atmosphere still hangs about the area. Despite its grandeur and beauty this has never quite departed.

The Harrison family of Henthorn Farm, 1870. The farm was situated in Pendle Witch Country.

When William Shakespeare, in his tragedy *Macbeth*, put 'Avaunt thee witch' into the mouth of 'the sailor's wife with chestnuts in her lap', he was speaking for England. Witches were greatly feared. In fact, the bard was hoping to curry favour with his sovereign James I, who relentlessly persecuted so-called witches and warlocks. He was also James VI of Scotland and decreed death in his treatise *Daemonologie* to any subject influenced by it.

Years ago, a tangible sign of those fearful times was discovered when a 400-year-old cruck-built thatched cottage was demolished.

Off I sped on a glorious day in June. Blue skies and hot sunshine prevailed while overhead billowing, white clouds like continents shunted across the azure blue, gently encouraged by a pleasant breeze. It was cycling weather. In those days amidst lanes lined with sweet smelling wild roses and hawthorn blossom, a mysterious stone had been found among rubble. As soon as the phone rang I began to thrill to the description of what I knew to be a Hag Stone, and sure enough it was.

The destruction of Jeff and Kath Morgan's cottage, built in the seventeenth century, had brought it to light. Beautifully shaped and smooth, a perfectly tactile oval, still retaining its green and ochre tints from the mosses and lichens applied three centuries ago, centrally placed and black outlined was the unmistakable drawing of an eye. This was the favourite defence, which appears again and again, in that classic stronghold of witches – Pendle Forest. 'Why?' you may ask.

Passed down in folklore was the belief that malevolent witches could harm crops, cattle, horses and people, ruin the harvest or turn milk sour. The hags, therefore, must be thwarted. When churning butter, a

A hag stone. The eye incised in the centre was known as 'the eye of God' and was thought to scare away witches. This one was found in the Fylde area when an old cottage was demolished.

silver coin was tossed. Farmers put one into the cheese press. Cottage industries were livelihoods and must be protected – flour, grain, butter, cheese, honey, salt were all considered vulnerable to evil.

Hag stones were one solution. Whistling was another so children were taught to whistle. It was thought that 'jingle bells' or wind chimes would keep a witch away, prevent her from entering barn, cottage, byre, mill, saltcote or dairy. Perhaps the intrinsic value of the hag stone was that all slept easier in their beds. Signs of the zodiac carved above the front door also were trusted weapons against witchcraft. I found these in Kirkby Lonsdale. Both Singleton and Poulton in the Fylde had individual methods in their amoury. Witness ducking stools beside ponds. In the heart of Lancashire the drama of witchcraft peaked in 1612 and before the year was out had played to its grim end.

The thirteen accused, terrified women were indeed a pathetic sight, dirty, ill-clad, mis-shapen, under-nourished. Poverty was rife in Pendle Forest. For the first time in their lives this motley crew were noticed and listened to by important people, unaware that they were incriminating themselves. Rivalry and family spite fuelled the fervour of biased magistrate and judges. Maybe the accused were a bad lot, liars and thieves, but they deserved help not death. They were mainly condemned on the evidence of a child.

Demdike, Chattox, Alison and Anne Redfern were sent for trial at Lancaster Assizes. Picture their journey under guard walking through the Trough of Bowland to incarceration in the blackness of Lancaster Castle's dungeons. In time the rest followed the same route apart from one Gisburn woman who was tried at York. Executions were carried out in public on 20 August. Old Demdike died in prison, blind and out of her mind.

In brilliant sunshine on that hot, summer's day it was uncanny to hold this ancient talisman and to conjure up the lives, voices and minds of ancestors who toiled, loved, wept, hated, laughed and walked in fear on the self-same plot of land so long ago.

Yet, to this day, Hallow'een 'rules, OK', sordidly but commercially sound.

Think 'Trick or Treat?'

Think Hag Stones!

CHAPTER TWELVE

My Name is Ozymandias!

Well it could have been, and that is better than 'Bighead' which is what the boys of Over-Wyre used to call the great stone inn sign of the Saracen's Head, Preesall. Old and genuine inn signs always interested me. In the years of our journeys to Cornwall whenever we reached the Norway Inn at Perranarworthal what a surge of joy – nearly there! The village of Point was our goal.

Every time I used to wonder Why Norway? What connection was there with this part of Britain and the Baltic? Curiosity was at last rewarded. At one time the creek nearby was navigable. Ships brought timber from Norway and took back lime. There is still an ancient lime kiln behind the Norway Inn.

The inn sign of the Saracen's Head, Preesall, no longer above the inn door. A tightrope walker used to perform on a highwire stretched from the inn to shops across the road. A dancing bear also visited with its keeper and they slept in the stable.

The Black Bull in our medieval market town once had a carved wooden figure of a bull hanging outside. It was so big the landlord used to sit astride it on traditional gala days when it was bedecked with ribbons. Such occasions date back over 100 years. Where is it now? Because Poulton was once a port, the Ship Inn had a model of a white-winged sailing ship swinging in the wind. That went years ago.

Some new signs enshrine history but unfortunately lack of information means that on occasions the depiction gets it wrong. In Lytham the Talbot Inn sign shows a Talbot dog. The original probably referred to Talbot Clifton, a local landowner! The inn signs that have welcomed wayfarers for centuries have been called 'Britain's finest free art collection'. In their day artists as famous as Hogarth and Morland painted them to eke out an existence.

One of the most expensive inn signs, costing £1,057 in 1655, was commissioned by John Peck, landlord at the White Hart at Scole in Norfolk. Supported by angels and lions, this sign, created by Fairchild, was designed to span the road. It included the coat of arms of twelve famous Norfolk families besides that of the landlord. There is so much history in old inn signs. For example, the many Red Lions are a legacy from James I who decided that public buildings should display the Scottish lion. The Green Man goes back to medieval times, the Jack in the Green of Merrie England festivals. Royal Oak must originate from the occasion when the king, who became Charles II, hid in an oak tree. The Three Willows in Hertfordshire is in an area famous for willows and cricket bat making since the eighteenth century.

Forty years ago there was a series of inn signs issued in colour on a set of cigarette cards – Wills' Passing Clouds. Out there at the Conventions there must be plenty of old postcards but to date I've found only one – the Trust Servant at Minstead in the New Forest, not far from the Rufus Stone.

One of the most magnificent signs in the Fylde countryside of Lancashire, indeed the whole country, was the great stone sign of the turbaned, bearded saracen placed above the door of the Saracen's Head at Preesall. A hundred years ago nobody knew how long he had been there, but in July 1943 'Bighead', as the locals called him, had to come down. The brewery company which owned the inn decided that in the interests of safety the saracen must be moved as his great weight was making the wall bulge. It took four workmen all day for the workmen to shift him by dint of chiselling the head away from the quaint recumbent figure on whose prostrate shoulders it rested. What was the ancient significance? It seemed to go back to the Crusades or to the days when pilgrims travelled to the Holy Land.

At the time no-one wanted him, not even the brewery company, until Jim Nicholson of Fernbreck Cottages housed the saracen in his garden. Passers-by in high wagonettes and early charabancs were curious to ask of his origins and village boys caused some damage to the saracen's beaky nose by leaning their bicycles against his stonework.

The Saracen's Head's original stone sign.

Such lack of interest in this ancient inn sign does illustrate how little people cared at the turn of the century for treasures which today would fetch hundreds of pounds and be fiercely defended. In the mid-twentieth century the sign did feature in a detective story 'Death Drops the Pilot', if only briefly, but it is interesting to note that four decades later another brewery company moved heaven and earth to regain possession.

No longer above the doorway as of yore, the hook-nosed, baleful-eyed, exotic traveller from an antique land, my Ozymandias, once more rests in the inn yard of his namesake, perhaps wondering how long he will be staying this time round. In order to reach Bighead country, the land where (according to brother Edward) the six spot burnet moth was sure to be seen, we crossed the River Wyre on one of the charming ferry boats leaving Fleetwood: *Playfair, Guarantee, Bourne May* and *Wyresdale* are names that come to mind. On less charming trips our boat could get stuck in the mud on a fast ebbing tide.

The boys loved the rotting signs of the defunct Knott End railway terminus. The last passenger train had pulled out in 1930. Like some of the ferry boats, the Pilling Pig engine was the butt of Over-Wyre jokes. Its whistle over the countryside was said to resemble the squeal of a dying pig and it was rumoured travel was so slow passengers could get out and pick flowers on the way. There are memories of home-made ice-cream bought at the Bourne Arms, an old inn, the refuge of shipwrecked sailors, and of

The ferry Wyresdale *preparing to set off for Knott End, across the River Wyre.*

course there were smuggling stories still circulating from another inn with atmosphere – the Ship, near Velvet Lane, so-called because bolts of French velvet and brandy were hurried up on dark nights from the lonely shore.

The weather always seemed to be sunny and there were marvellous views across Morecambe Bay to the Lake District mountains, all of which was more alluring to us than the Big Wheel or the Tower at Blackpool.

CHAPTER THIRTEEN

Foudroyant & Other Trips

On a perfect summer's day in June 1897 Father and Grandfather set off from their hill-top village, Belthorn, above Blackburn, to make what was then quite a journey. Travelling by the Preston and Wyre steam railway, for the last five miles they had cantered over Fylde moss-land in a high wagonette, arriving at Blackpool as the sun went down. The news that Lord Nelson's historic flagship, the *Foudroyant*, was anchored off the town had travelled fast and like thousands more they wanted to see her.

In her day one of the most famous ships in the world, it was strange indeed that the country's number one playground by the sea should be the scene of her memorable wrecking.

For a fortnight the vessel, anchored three miles off North and Central Piers, was an object of interest to thousands of holidaymakers. Steamers and sailing craft had daily conveyed people to tread the decks and explore the Admiral's Cabin. 'Flaming, thunderous, firestriking' was the meaning of the name of this most renowned of the wooden-walled ships of the old British Navy, and she had lived up to it, making history under the greatest naval hero of all time, Horatio Nelson. Launched in the spring of 1798 at Plymouth and christened after a captured French ship, *Foudroyant* was a sixty-gun two-decker. Lord St Vincent wrote to Nelson: 'She is the most perfect ship that ever swam on salt water.' Standing on her decks, the unparalleled Admiral had made his greatest chase of the *Genereux*, urging the Captain to 'crowd on every stitch of canvas and make the *Foudroyant* fly to the capture'.

Twice in her career the ship was a refuge for the Royal families of Naples and Portugal. Fleeing from Napoleon, a sister of Marie Antoinette had hidden on board. The recovery of Malta also figured in the vessel's distinguished career.

Although in 1851 *Foudroyant* was extensively repaired, the sad day dawned when the ruthless Admiralty decision, 'sold out of service to a Plymouth ship breaker', was announced. To save her from the even greater ignominy of being towed to Germany for firewood, rich man Mr G.W. Cobb stepped in. He spent £20,000 on refitting *Foudroyant*, planning to exhibit her at many seaside resorts. Following a spell at Southport it was arranged that she would be Blackpool's greatest attraction in Queen Victoria's Diamond Jubilee Year, 1897. Fate provided a town which gloried in the spectacular with one of the most sensational occurrences in its eventful history.

In Nelson's day *Foudroyant* had a crew of 713 but as a show ship she was in the charge of 6 men and 20 lads, the latter dressed as jolly Jack Tars. Fooled by blue skies, Captain William John Robins paid no heed to warnings that if the wind rose the *Foudroyant* could be in difficulty.

After a good Lancashire high tea, Clement and Edward, the latter one of a number who feared Captain Robins was courting disaster, walked to the beach. Clement, a mere boy, was to talk of the *Foudroyant*'s wrecking for the rest of his days. He told me: 'We saw her the night before the storm looking picturesque with her masts and rigging all trim and neat, her painted portholes looking like black and white tile work. The setting of a calm sea was reminiscent of the old, romantic days of sea battles, when the great wooden ships came to grips with the French.'

Unexpected and unannounced, the gale began that evening and by early morning sailings on the *Queen of the North* and for the Isle of Man were

The spectacular wrecking of Lord Nelson's flagship Foudroyant *off Blackpool, 1897. The wreck was witnessed by my father.* Foudroyant *timbers were made into souvenirs including jewel boxes, tables and walking-sticks, while oak and copper salvaged from the wreck were used to make Masonic lodge furniture.*

cancelled. Local historian Allen Clarke heard the wind howling amidst chimney pots. 'There came a man with the news that *Foudroyant* had broken loose from its moorings and was drifting ashore. As I dashed out of doors I could see she was already aground, level with the Hotel Metropole. *Foudroyant* lay on her beam ends, huge waves sweeping her decks, watched by a seething mass of human faces concentrating on the death struggle.'

Cracking like whips, first one then another of her three masts snapped and toppled overboard, carrying yards and spars with them until only three stumps remained. For six hours the fate of the crew was uncertain but suddenly men were seen crawling towards the shelter of the poop deck. Borne slowly on the tide, it had been feared that the massive vessel would sweep away the Pier Jetty, but this was mercifully averted by the current moving northwards.

Wheatley Cobb, writing to his mother from the Wellington Hotel, described how it had looked from the ship. 'Floods of water swept through the shattered door of the Admiral's cabin. I had never seen waves like them . . . no one could have lived two minutes in that sea. Every internal fitting and bulkhead was swept away, the decks rent to pieces, timbers ripped in every direction and she bumped with such violence that the lower deck guns ploughed grooves three feet deep through the solid oak sides of the ship . . . A shout went up that the new lifeboat had put out. We got into the *Samuel Fletcher* and were landed in a crowd of several thousands.'

Meanwhile Blackpool's enterprising advertising manager C. Nadin was busy telegraphing the news all over the country, bringing in trainloads of sightseers in search of souvenirs.

My father found copper nails. Much of the wonderful timber was carted off and made into furniture, walking sticks, jewel boxes, while metal was melted down to become commemorative medallions, many of which survive.

Mr Cobb employed a salvage company from Glasgow, striking an agreement that if the Company failed to refloat *Foudroyant* they could have the ship for £10 and be paid nothing. The guns and beautifully carved figurehead were recovered, the latter being preserved at Caldicott Castle, but the attempt to refloat was a failure.

Strangely enough, the unique *Foudroyant* had still not had the last word. Two further vessels were wrecked trying to salvage more timber and in the following November another raging sea smashed what remained of *Foudroyant* to bits, dismembering every oak plank and beam.

According to Grandfather, and maybe even Nelson himself would have agreed along with other old salts in that huge crowd, it was fitting that such a great ship should bow out at the height of storm and tempest.

Few knew more of west coast sea lore than Grandfather. 'The old warrior fought to the last,' he said, unsurprised that after sailing the seven seas for a century, Nelson's 'Dear *Foudroyant*' had finally been conquered by the furious capability of the Irish Sea.

Talking of trips, although there wasn't much 'brass' to spare for our generation, mother seemed to work wonders in the way of food and outings, investing both with her rich store of imagination. I loved her lemon curd and the way she thinly sliced big jaffa oranges, layering them with sugar in a deep, cut-glass dish. Father was a great storyteller, especially when the rice pudding course came on. 'Eat up and I'll tell you a Jimmy Eccles story,' he would say, Jimmy Eccles having been his bosom pal. The stories were always about Belthorn, the village where he was born. One tale was so very long that one toddler fell fast asleep with her golden curls in the pudding and the bowl.

I only ever remember accompanying Father on one picnic. Typically he chose the depths of winter when, on the spur of the moment, he had decided to take his two little girls in search of 'a utick's nest.' Needless to say, we never found it, but I still remember the mystery and the magic he wove into that trip to Heaton Park. We settled by a tree stump and 'laid the table', spreading out our drinks, cake, fruit and sandwiches. Well wrapped up like two scarlet balls, my sister and I have no recollection of feeling cold.

One of the many bands who played during Peace Day celebrations after the First World War. During hostilities, in 1916, a Zeppelin passed over Stacksteads and my father and his cousin Sam Lord climbed through a fanlight and watched it from the roof. This was no mean feat when one considers Father only had one good leg. The other was crippled by what was then known as infantile paralysis.

May Day revels were dying out when we were little. A survival of the festival in honour of the goddess of spring and in rejoicing that the rigours of winter were over, after hundreds of years' practice came down to our street in the shape of torn, old lace curtains, wooden, half hoops decorated with paper flowers, scraps of satin ribbon, whatever the mothers could rustle up in those hard times, but to us children they were gorgeous trappings. Imagination went a long way. We sang lustily about 'crowning the Queen of the May' and even the boys joined in, blacking their faces and becoming 'coconut men'. Although I didn't know it, in ages past our village, Rooden Lane, had been renowned for its 'bringing in the May' and for the care put into it.

The coming of spring still had great significance. Friends and relatives flocked into town and a day of rejoicing and reunion. Easter Monday meant a trek up Holcombe Hill and some pace egging, which people must have done for 'donkeys' years'. It was something to look forward to. Nowadays families go off in the car as on any old weekend.

People were then still very superstitious. I remember being shocked when told that on no account must I take a twig of sweetly smelling hawthorn into the house or it would cause my mother to die. Planned in my childish way as a lovely surprise, you may guess my feelings when it so miserably backfired. Some of the superstitions went back to pagan times. 'The cat is raising the wind,' said Grandmother, when Tiger tore at the furniture with his claws. If a cat died in the house that was bad luck, but if a black kitten walked in that was good luck. As we had three cats there was a good chance of either. Among these wiseacre sayings, weather figured largely:

> If Rivington Pike do wear a hood,
> Be sure the day will ne'er be good.

and

> When Pendle wears its woolly cap,
> The farmers all may take a nap.

We found most true the following:

> When clouds appear like rocks and towers,
> The earth's refreshed by constant showers.

Our prayers always finished with the verse we were taught to say at that point. I have since found out that it was common practice in many parts of Lancashire and no doubt mother herself, grandmother and great-grandmother had all been taught likewise. So much was passed on from mother to daughter, father to son.

> Matthew, Mark, Luke and John,
> Bless the bed that I lie on.

An exciting spectacle for us in summer was to watch the rooks flying overhead at sunrise to their rookery at the Grand Lodge. There were hundreds of them that appeared at a given time, darkening the sky, and it took many minutes for the flock to pass over. One day Edward brought a raven home. It had an injured wing. He, who loved all birds and living creatures, had found it at the foot of a tree after a spell of wild, windy weather. It perched on his shoulder, black, sinister-looking, with its long,

Edward, my eldest brother, 'went for a soldier' as soon as the Second World War broke out in 1939. He had been hankering to set off for the Spanish Civil War. A young man full of ideals and old-fashioned chivalry, he soon became disenchanted, but retained his love of birds and animals to the end. A lecturer at a military college of science and later employed at the Radar Research Establishment at Malvern, Edward specialised on birdstrike, which minimised hazard to aircraft from flocks of birds. He wrote a paper for the magazine Nature *on the subject.*

sharp, yellow beak close to his face. He and the bird trusted each other implicitly and were quite relaxed, but my parents were afraid and insisted Edward take it back to the foot of the same tree. It must have broken Edward's heart to walk all that way back and abandon it, but he obeyed.

Cock fighting was officially a thing of the past, but Father told stories about Great-Grandfather's visits to Kersal moor where in the eighteenth century there was even a ladies' stand on the racecourse. A cock-match between the gentlemen of Yorkshire and the gentlemen of Lancashire was held after the racing.

We had day trips to Blackpool and to Southport where Grandma Houghton, by now a very old lady, had retired. I remember the diamond-patterned tiles of Saunders Street and the first bag of shrimps I ever tasted at Southport: tangy, savoury, overhung with the salt scent of the sea. We also loved trips to the markets of Bury, Burnley, Chorley, Prestwich, Accrington, where I recall the pungent scent of celery hearts and displays of sausages and black puddings.

The great wheel at Blackpool was a major attraction in the early years of the twentieth century. It was dismantled in about 1923. The whole family went on the great wheel just as today the populace uses the London Eye.

Catherine, Edward and Charles on a trip to Blackpool in 1925.

The family on donkeys at Blackpool seventy years ago. Though many years have passed since my father took this photograph, I still recall that my donkey was called Maggie. All the Blackpool donkeys had names and spent the winters in Poulton fields.

The best thing about Southport Pier was the long ride to the end on a train which had real railway carriages. As a small child I recall the terror of going down the iron steps with the sea raging underneath. When we got to the end of the pier Grandma always wanted to go to the loo and Mother and I had to escort her.

Delivering fruit to Southport Market. On Saturday evenings, as markets closed, 'dinged' or damaged fruit could be bought very cheaply as otherwise over the weekend it grew mouldy and became useless. All kinds of fruit – redcurrants, blackcurrants, bilberries – were made into delicious pies for Sunday dinner. Especially I recall the purple bilberries that Mother made into pies which stained lips and teeth – whereupon we four children would grin widely at each other, displaying purple tongues like chow dogs.

Father being a travelling photographer, we did get around. For a time he had a photographic studio at Waterfoot, close to Lewis Nuttall's shop. Carved chairs with barley-sugar-shaped spindle backs gravitated from there to the spartan two-up, two-down cottage where we lived, an unusual mix with scrubbed linoleum, scrubbed table top and Great Uncle Jonathan's oil paintings on the walls. There were other small items of beauty (among the stone jam jars pressed into service for containers) and these made a difference to our lives, enriching the commonplace. I recall delicious Sunday lunches in early spring, with a bunch of paper-white, scented narcissi on the table and a delicate, blue, glass water jug embossed with white marguerites.

Pendle Hill, near Clitheroe. 'Here to the bone are my beginnings.' To this day the area reeks of the true Lancashire heartland and I love it. I remember it in all weathers: shrouded in autumn mist; etched clear against the sky in summer; its great bluff shouldering starkly in icy winter just before the all-enveloping fog hid it from sight. The Lancashire witches added nothing for me. Great Pendle always spoke for itself.

Best of all we loved the country, walking on the Pennine hills, going 'over the tops' from Edenfield and dropping down into Rossendale valley, climbing from Downham, following the old Roman road beyond Holcombe or questing around Clitheroe Castle and Whalley Abbey. Our first kingfisher was seen by the bridge at Dunsop, a never-to-be-forgotten streak of fire and sapphire against the rich, brown, wet earthiness of the river bank, where we also watched water boatmen skimming the surface, mayflies, dragonflies, and in the shallows, paddling in our bare feet, constructed dams out of the clay.

All this seasonal activity seemed to work up to the most exciting time of all – Christmas, with its free shows in the shops.

On Christmas Show Night shopkeepers competed with each other to make the mouth water. Fish, geese, turkeys, ducks, rabbits, hares and all kinds of game and venison crammed the most up-to-date premises in town, but I hated to see the scrubbed, pink pigs so dead with big oranges popped

Tomlinson and Shepherd, two young Haslingden playmates in their usual attire, including the ever-present clogs.

The village of Hambleton in 1902. Christmas supplies came from a number of farms here: pork, beef, geese, ducks and chickens.

into their gaping mouths, sometimes from which rolled a thin trickle of blood. I liked the chemist's shop with its three enormous Winchester bottles of coloured liquids glowing blue, red and yellow alongside a huge pestle and mortar.

We gazed long and big-eyed at the toyshop windows in Manchester, knowing full well we would never see such magnificence in our home at Christmas. Well, a cat could look at a king!

CHAPTER FOURTEEN

Station in Life

Iremember watching from the wall a line of railway coaches stretching to below where I stood and under the bridge and beyond, and the last coach had not emerged from the tunnel at the further end of the platform. Hundreds of figures in khaki loaded with personal baggage, standing in groups, and the long, long time the train took to move off from the empty platform, for by then the men had gone. I remember being told that a famous locomotive, *The Great Bear*, might pass by on that line – though now I think such an event would have been unlikely – and the keen disappointment I felt when it failed to appear. The General Strike was an interesting time when the railwaymen joined the miners to protest against cuts in wages that the government was forcing upon these workers. No proper trains ran for some days. True, an unexpected locomotive or two appeared on the line through long intervals of time, but there seemed to be a certain lack of expertise on the part of the driving staff, made up, I believe, of black-leg labour drawn from engineering students at the local university. The boilers ran out of steam frequently and firing was amateurish, and consequently timetables could by no means be relied upon, nor could the service. What I did notice was the long time the signal lamps remained alight with no attention, never had they been left so long unattended, and the reader must understand that signal lights were never extinguished apart from the brief time needed to trim and refill with oil.

Beneath our kitchen window stood the platelayer's hut, where in foggy weather detonators placed on the up line before the passage of each train exploded at regular time-intervals, and depending on the foulness of the fog the resultant sound varied from a resounding bang to a muffled bump. In the insalubrious atmosphere of freezing cold, sometimes with snow, and sulphurous mustard yellow smog, the platelayer at his brazier kept his vigil, a dim shadow behind the ruby glow of burning coke, while water distilled in drops on each piece of ice-cold metal exposed to the open air. Noisome air swirled around, irritating mucous membranes of nose and throat, and tiring pink-rimmed eyes. The fog forced its way into buildings everywhere, especially where the temperature was low, but even into dwelling houses it insinuated by way of ill-fitting doors and windows, rotting the Nottingham lace curtains and causing them to give off an odour of ammonia on washday as they sank beneath the thrice-renewed soapsuds.

Britannia Pacific 4–6–2 Oliver Cromwell *at Thornton Cleveleys station.*

But oh the porters' room on late Friday afternoons! Spit and polish in whitewood tabletop and the wooden forms drawn up alongside, all scrubbed like a butcher's counter. Concrete floor swabbed with very hot, soapy water strongly laced with tar oil disinfectant, and the step and fire surround tinted with cream donkey stone, fire range newly blackleaded with highlights of polished steel. The windows were freshly washed and polished and there were opal glass lampshades. And such a delicious smell from the fire oven of baked potatoes, or the occasional warming-up of a recently cooked meal waiting for some guard who intended to finish his shift at that station. As the evening advanced a pair of oil hand lamps were lit and stood in a prominent place, and the coal scuttle, topped up with best coal from the bunker outside, was brought in and placed near the fire. Two single rings on the bell – that's the signalman – take his can of water before dusk and then we are ready for the evening and the longer waits between trains.

Our station received parcels but had no goods yard: nothing larger than a basket of racing pigeons or a milk churn was accepted there, though the station at the village next along boasted its coal yard with bays, goods warehouse, loading gauge and stationary crane with wooden jib which never seemed to be put to use. It also had a passenger siding referred to as 'The Bay', and from which vantage point one could watch the local cricket team play in summer without payment.

To where was the rolling stock of those days finally shunted? Where did it terminate its working life? First, the wooden coal trucks, ten or twelve tons capacity, with manually applied brakes, most of them seemingly to have seen their last coat of paint decades before my time. The name of each coal company was painted on each wagon: 'Butterly', read one, 'Staveley', another. There were so many names and there were the other purpose-built trucks or vans, fish or fruit, or double length wooden louvred milk vans from Scotland. Then those proprietary vans, 'Colmans' or 'Cerebos', and later 'Fyffes', each designed for the job in hand.

I wonder how many different designs of guard's van existed in the days of steam. There seemed to be so many variations on the single theme: some squat with an open platform at one end and running on two pairs of wheels and some longer ones mounted on three pairs of wheels. All, however, had that indispensable chimney protruding through the roof, more often than not with a thin wisp of blue smoke trailing behind. Each side of the van, too, had observation slits with glass panes through which the guard could watch front and rear of the train. There was a time when I envied the goods guard, for he must have been a fortunate man with no passengers to chivvy on the train nor wellwishers to warn away from the platform edge; no mailbags to hinder his time schedule nor packages to delay his passage. He had not even the easy task of ejecting a bundle of town newspapers onto a country platform. He was utterly dependent on the driver for the speed of the goods he carried and on the acumen of the signalman for the alacrity of his passing from section to section (bearing in mind also the regulations of the railway company). What did this most fortunate man do to while away the time? Obviously he must have stood against the steel bar barrier outside his cabin, watching the scenery pass between straight track and curve, cutting the embankment, incline and descent, girder bridge, tunnel and brick viaduct as the locomotive puffed steadily on its way mile after mile. When this palled, or when he was hungry or the weather was wet or otherwise inclement, or when night had fallen, he betook him to the glowing stove within, to refuel and warm himself or to cook thereon an abundance of sizzling gammon rashers, lying alongside a couple of orange-yoked eggs and brown fingers of fried bread. Later a pint pot or two of hot, sweet tea and a following pipe of fragrant tobacco. Beyond lighting his lamp what else could he have had to do?

And our station nowadays? 'Passengers must not cross the line except by the bridge,' the original notice still reads. It is one of the few things that have not altered in all these years, when so much else has. Crossing that bridge I look down on the carriage roof on which infinitesimal fragments of steel thrown off by friction between high tension cable and pantograph have oxidised in the rain. Driblets of water blown into crazy patterns at high speed stagger along, rusty brown, to the rear. The sound of motion is different: there's no longer the endless deh-deh, deh-dey–de-deh, deh-dey–de-deh, deh-deh to lull one into a state of quiescence. Never again will we hear the comforting rhythm of the wheels as they traverse the lengths of steel track for nowadays rails are continuous strips of steel. No longer is there a leather strap to release a window to absorb the smell of burning coal from the engine, for warm and well-lit carriages now cosset us from the elements outside.

CHAPTER FIFTEEN

Trial by Gaslight

A vivid portrayal of schooldays emerges
from my brother Charles's recollections.

Across the street from Big Croft was the school. The Senior part was nearest the lower playground, and the Infants above the Three Steps in a more restricted space. Some of my earliest memories stem from here. There was the kindergarten schoolroom with its cheerful fire in winter, protected by a big, brass-railed fireguard. Here the alphabet was held aloft in the monitor's hand, letter following letter in the usual sequence and repeated by the little ones until known. Even now I can remember the rectangles of pink card with the letter complete with serifs in indian ink. Here, too, were the little tables and chairs and the rocking horse that was purchased the term we left the room so that we never had a ride. Bowls of bulbs in spring brightened the surroundings and here was the reed organ for sustaining infant voices of indeterminate pitch, one of which I still recall:

> Come, little leaves,' said the wind one day,
> Come o'er the meadows with me, and play;
> Put on your dresses of red and gold;
> Summer is gone, and the days grow cold.

And now another one has come to mind:

> Master North Wind's blowing, Ooooh . . .
> Through the forest he is going, Ooooh . . .
> Can't you hear his voice so shrill,
> Can't you hear him whistle still,
> Master North Wind's blowing, Oooo . . .

The teacher wore a blouse and a long, certainly well below the knee, skirt in Donegal tweed and a large wristlet watch, leather encased, which she told us once belonged to her brother who had died not that many years before in the trenches of Flanders. From here we went to the second class in the Big Room with its painted brick walls. From the wooden skirting was three feet of dark green gloss, two inches of black and to the ceiling the rest in light cream gloss. There was plaster only on the ceiling and tiles were non-existent, and I think I am right in saying that the walls were repainted every three years.

In this second class, with its four sides of blanket stitch round a rectangle of dark blue paper, with its raffia teapot stands and the initiation into those mysterious 'tables' we had heard so much about, we were also introduced to drawing. We began by making a drawing of the teacher's smart red handbag and the desks ran scarlet that day. We sat at two-seater desks which had slate slots, though slates were before my time, and almost every subject was performed in them except a species of simple, unexciting PE, without apparatus, called 'Drill'. Our hand work now included hair tidies 'to hang on mother's dressing table', and the beginning of paper models planned from the flat. Whenever bored, and there were times, one tried to relieve the monotony by glancing round the walls at the framed illustrations from Barrie's *Peter Pan* by Mabel Lucie Attwell, or cogitating on the framed presentation shield hung above the central fireplace. We were not told a single fact about it, so we simply took it for granted and made no effort to find out.

And so to Junior class one, though the notice, cloth on rollers, said Regulations of the Public Elementary School, or some such.

Junior class one was in Lower School below Three Steps and the lower playground. This part of the school was in charge of a headmaster. There we saw him but a few months – and then no more. That a child should die, through chances and hazards we knew. One of the better-dressed boys in my class, he wore brown wellingtons (which were then, I think, a new idea for children), had to come daily over the fields which were often wet in winter, and had the misfortune to catch meningitis. Later we were told he had died. About the same time that winter another, poorer boy caught diphtheria, quite common then, with its companion scarlet fever, and he too succumbed. For a teacher to cease suddenly to be in school when we were not told that he had left to take another job seemed awfully strange and something to wonder at. Then we were told that he had died suddenly. Later we were asked to contribute a copper or two as a school gesture to a memorial wreath. Later still the older pupils were led to the graveyard half a mile away to view the red granite memorial stone that had been erected over his grave.

In the short time I saw this headmaster I was quite overawed. He was one of the old-fashioned type in which all material should, if possible, be turned into an example or lesson somewhat on the Chinese idea that one picture is worth a thousand words. His class and school discipline was wonderful to behold; he had but to turn his head to any direction for silence to fall immediately. I rather doubt if he ever was an approachable person – he was the essence of Victorian authority.

The week I moved to the Lower School a boy who had stepped out of line was to be shown the error of his ways, not merely corrected or summarily punished by caning, but brought before the whole school and there displayed as the 'awful example' from which we must ever flee. It seemed to be more of an exercise, less of a punitive retribution than a re-enactment of the way the dread law dealt with condemned criminals in Newgate in the eighteenth and early nineteenth centuries. Let us remember that it was rare for a child raised during the second half of Victoria's reign to be allowed the slightest deviation from the path laid out for it: bear in mind that the only book usually allowed for the child's reading on Sundays, apart from the Bible and assuming he was not a Roman Catholic, was that grim horror *Foxe's Book of Martyrs*, illustrated. To continue: a bell rang fifteen minutes before the end of afternoon school and one by one in silence classes marched into the Hall, there to stand erect in columns before the small platform, which was to do duty as a 'scaffold'. The teachers neatly arranged themselves round the wall and a senior boy lit the gas lamps (since, it being late December, the room was now becoming dark), which he did with a taper affixed to a map pole. The 'malefactor', rather than naughty child, entered immediately followed by the headmaster and in that order they mounted the place of 'execution'. The closing hymn of the day was announced, and from memory the children sang, verses five and six being appropriate to the crime committed:

> When deep within our swelling hearts
> The thoughts of pride and anger rise,
> When bitter words are on our tongues,
> And tears of passion in our eyes;
>
> Then we may stay the angry blow
> Then we may check the hasty word,
> Give gentle answers back again,
> And fight a battle for our Lord.

All this time the condemned stood alone at one end of the platform with lowered head and dejected mein while justice in bald head, walrus moustache, winged collar and *pince-nez* stood at the other. The hymn finishing and the closing prayer read, an anticipatory silence fell as the headmaster advanced to the small table and faced the school with his right forefinger resting on the table edge. He sternly read the indictment and as he stressed the seriousness of the misdemeanour and sentence was pronounced the children, if possible, grew more quiet then ever. 'Come here, boy: hold out your right hand.' The boy faltered and then advanced, and the cane discreetly hidden by the table was now raised to full view. He flinched as the first blow struck but dumbly carried out instruction as the headmaster continued, 'And now the other hand.' For full theatrical effect it would have been better with muffled drums but the dramatic silence, now broken by cries from the weeping child, caused the young audience to glance with horror at the Jack Ketch standing above his victim. The master went on, 'And now turn your face to the wall: your name will be written in the Black Book.' In silence we were dismissed. Let us, therefore, move over to my class.

In my school uniform the year I won my scholarship. I gained top marks in the whole of Lancashire.

In this class for the one and only time at school I was teacher's blue-eyed pupil – I simply couldn't go wrong, except once! On that occasion I was beaten by a boy I had never considered a rival. He was Cecil, yes Cecil, and he was blonde, slim, spoke well, had clean buffed nails and impeccable manners. In comparison I was a non-starter. In addition to his pious appearance he would think nothing, if the teacher suggested it, of singing the alternate verses of 'The Keys of Canterbury' while facing a girl of the class who sang the other verses. Worse still, he would with his left arm raised and right palm pressed to his heart, kneel before the blushing damsel and sing in his clear treble that he would give the keys of his heart and be married till death do us part . . . Which girl partner didn't seem to matter one iota; had I been vigorously pushed and my arm well twisted I, perhaps, would have considered singing a verse or two to Freda, who had shining brown bobbed hair, freckles and dimples and always a lovely smile, but not kneeling. Perhaps even Bernice of the heart shaped face and springy auburn curls, too, but Cecil would elegantly genuflect which girl stood before him, and without any prompting, showed no partisan feeling in the matter. My position sank still lower when he freely volunteered to sing at an Open Day a sentimental and high toned ditty called 'My Task', that repeated the strain 'And Smile When Evening Falls' in a most convincing rendition, while looking up to heaven like the picture of an Italian saint in a Catholic repository. He left school soon afterwards and no one took his place. When Cecil left I was free again to continue my course without rivalry: seldom did I fall below the top of the class in the weekly tests, for I led in arithmetic and practically everything else. I served my teacher with complete devotion – even now with so many years past I consider her a great teacher. She certainly knew how to get me to work.

Pride goeth . . . in the next class I fell from grace. I could not appreciate the dry wit of the middle-aged spinster in charge. Contrarily, my brother got on like a house on fire and did very well. Only in one thing did I make good progress in her class, and it was something not taught in the school – I became acting (unpaid) school pianist for I was better at playing piano than any of the teaching staff, but that wasn't saying a great deal. One thing she did teach me and most of the other children was singing from Tonic Sol-fa, eventually from sight, an accomplishment that is not strong in British schools nor has been for forty years or more, and that was no small thing, speaking as a musician.

Parish pump patriotism was still in full spate in school, even so soon after the 'war to end all wars', and it was poured over us by the panful, in history, in poetry and in song. There seemed to be no end to it: There's a Land a Dear Land; Three Cheers for the Red, White and Blue; Ye Mariners of England; Hearts of Oak; Kipling's Recessional, Land of our Birth; Our England is a Garden; If; Puck of Pook's Hill; The Arethusa; together with the inescapable Land of Hope and Glory and great dollops of Sir Henry Newbolt and like-minded poets.

It was a common act for the whole school to parade in the playground and for the boys to march past and salute the flag on Empire Day, marching by in twos and forming fours for inspection. When one schoolgirl wrote an essay 'Why I am Proud to be British' or some such in rather jingoistic terms and had been greatly criticised by a visiting HM Inspector with broader views, the partisan *Daily Mail* sold many more copies with their write up on the case.

And so to the last teacher of that school, the headmaster himself, not the one of my earlier years but a younger man who also lived with his cane within easy reach, but was more uncertain in its use! He took a divided class, the greater part of whom intended to leave at the age of fourteen, and a tiny set being coached for the few county scholarships in the county with the largest population. I was in the latter section. Each day invariably began with the headmaster taking down a cane – it was kept hanging on a prominent place on the wall – and with it flailing the nearest desk crying: 'Fireworks, that's what we're going to have today. And a free show of fireworks for all who haven't remembered.' I would look through the high class room windows, gently moving my head from left to right to see the house chimneys opposite ripple like a belly dancer through the varying thickness of the glass. Barbara hid her confused mind in a useless ploy that all her classmates knew was unavailing – she developed a shocking cough within seconds of the lesson beginning. Then there was Annie. She was, without doubt, Deirdre of the Sorrows and daily entered school weeping, being daily thirty minutes later, carrying in her relaxed hand some pathetic floral tribute to the teacher, be it buttercups and daisies or daffodils. Auburn haired, feckless Annie, heaven only knows why she came to our school since she was very Irish and a Roman Catholic. 'Indian wives resort to suttee in their country on the deaths of their husbands. Why, and who stamped out suttee in India?' The small, usual band of 'didn't know' began to wend its way to the front of the class, hands at the ready – to be caned! You've done it before and you'll do it again, so why bother; let's get it over; you can't win in this game. The clichés and the conjecture without a shred of foundation and the claptrap surmise rapidly gleaned from the 'popular' press, how often did we hear it? The personal likes and dislikes; the unsubstantiated newspaper reportage and real facts thrown out together; pure water polluted by seepage from a less wholesome source. Scepticism developed. There was not much enjoyment here, and at last when I gained a county scholarship I left with no regrets.

CHAPTER SIXTEEN

Tom Mix & the Art Gallery

While I was a girl, the cinema or kinema as Arthur Mee (editor of the long defunct *Children's Newspaper* and *Children's Pictorial*), would have it, was growing in popularity. These grand halls of rich magnificence and most doubtful architectural pedigree were springing up all over the land offering two-and-a-half hours of dreamworld entertainment at low cost. Because of the last consideration we attended perhaps once a fortnight in our most enamoured period, and thereafter as the years passed we went less and less until it became an occasional change in the way we spent our leisure time.

Even the way to the local picture house could, or perhaps one day would, lead to adventure, or so we often hoped! Skirting the steam laundry where the gas engine blasted its exhaust beneath a double layer of corrugated iron sheeting and shaking the immediate earth as we passed down the bank, we advanced along the sandy track suitable only for children since there were two four foot fences to climb before the Brow (pronounced Brew). Alongside the stream issuing from a railway cutting culvert flooding in heavy downpour, the path continued over a clapper bridge of gritstone and alongside the blue painted palings to a leafy, country lane. Then the dingle, site of the old Rectory in the fifteenth and sixteenth centuries, where golden fluffy male flowers of Great Sallow smoked yellow pollen as one brushed by them about Eastertide. There was also an ancient draw well where we would often sit round the edge fully ten feet in diameter, dangling our bare knees (boys don't seem to have knees nowadays; they are always shielded from the elements by cloth). Mercifully the well was dry and about four feet deep, for none of us could swim. Beyond was 'no man's pasture' where a ragged and dishevelled man existed in a hovel of random planks, sacking, old tarpaulin and beaten iron sheeting. With him dwelt his rough pelted horse and neither seemed to work in the way society expects. We called him The Hermit. He didn't encourage visitors, especially children. Only one big field to pass through, where the annual circus rested, directed by Lord John Sanger and supporting the usual lions and tigers and an inordinate number of elephants, or so it seemed to me. Then at last, our goal, the

Picturedrome. The entrance fee for one child to the first house was *2d* and with an added ½d one could buy a stick of Everton toffee and make it a night out.

I cannot hope to enumerate and name all, or even a tiny fraction of those silent cinematograph shows we sat through, but they may yet appear on television. Tom Mix the cowboy was one of our heroes, although, shameful of me, I have forgotten the name of his faithful steed. The name Starlight hovers around. Buster Keaton and Harold Lloyd amused; Lon Chaney terrified; Douglas Fairbanks thrilled, especially in films like *The Mark of Zorro*. Films like Conrad's *Nostromo*, Wilder's *The Bridge of San Luis Rey*, Blasco-Ibanez's *The Four Horsemen of the Apocalypse* or any of Maugham's filmed novels appealed because of their action; the psychological patterns were quite lost on us. Gorky's *Mother* was a film like no other. Its real people (rather than paper figures) saddened; its gloom and grey drabness appalled and long it stayed in my memory.

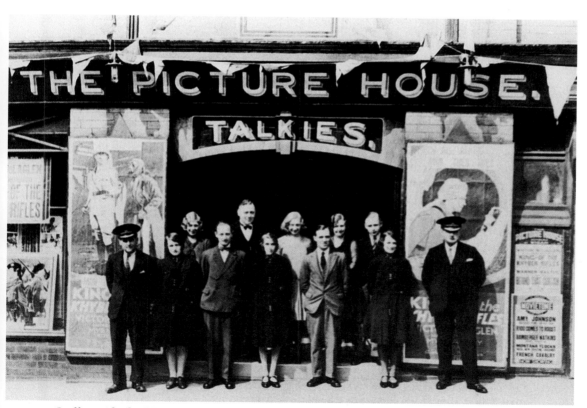

Staff outside the Wigan Cinema on the day 'talkies' came to their picture house, September 1929. Around this time a song was written which became a popular gramophone record: 'If I had a talking picture of you'.

Belphagor was a weekly cliff-hanger as was also *The Iron Maiden* and those repetitive Sax Rohmer Dr Fu Manchu series that lasted week after week, month after month, until one stayed away for sheer boredom. We saw several versions of *A Yankee at King Arthur's Court* – the Will Rogers one was the best, I thought, and the mechanised steeds contributed by the Yankee in the earliest version. Motor cycles had developed into Austin Sevens in the last. *The Hunchback of Notre Dame* and *Beau Geste* also were directed more than once.

There was another cinema two miles along the road known among the coarser rustics and vulgar little boys as 'The Fleapit' or 'Bughouse'. It was a noisy place and the clientele was not so select as in the Picturedome. True, one could gain entrance to a Saturday matinee in the first five rows of seats for as little as one penny, old coinage, but throughout the performance there could be a shower of orange peel falling on the righteous and unrighteous alike and we were strongly discouraged by our parents from attending, or, if we did then we dare not complain. We did go, and thus had a penny left over to buy a bottle of 'pop' with a black vulcanite screw stopper. Dearer mineral water cost about 3*d* and had to be shared since its exorbitant cost ruled out one apiece. These superior bottles had a dimpled neck and the pressure of the gas within was held by a glass marble. This pressure was overcome by forcing the 'alley' to the middle of the neck and so permitting gas to escape together with the beverage. Oh, the dandelion and burdock, the American ice cream soda, the lemonade we consumed! Eventually we forsook those coloured, flavoured and sweetened powders, euphemistically called Lemonade and Raspberryade. Even with dilution I never liked them, nor, for that matter, was I wildly enthusiastic about kali or sherbet powder. Some children took tiger nuts and liquorice root to chew, but they were hard to come by in our area. Peanuts (ex-shells) were 'coming-in' then, and monkey nuts became more scarce.

Now and again we would travel to the further cinema by tram, and that meant no sweets or pop. Two nearby towns used electricity for their transport on the two main roads, chiefly tramcars, though there were a few electric trolley buses, which were still a novelty and none came anywhere near our village. The smaller town, less affluent, had a route passing The Street and Butterthorn Lane and this was the one we used. The bigger town, which was more important, and richer, could use trams of the largest size, indeed they were the largest I saw anywhere. They had four wheel bogies at the front and the rear, instead of the usual four spaced wheels, and had also in consequence a smoother ride. They were totally enclosed from the weather, had upholstered seats downstairs and passed magnificently down the thoroughfare looking like nothing less than gigantic illuminated glass panelled display cabinets. Moreover, each tram had a trolley boy, in addition to the two man team of driver and conductor. To the simple onlooker the job of trolley boy, a trainee youth, seemed to consist chiefly of moving the trailing power pole to the rear of the vehicle when either terminus was reached. On the other hand 'our trams' were

The Friargate, Preston, in the early years of the twentieth century.

more primitive, had holed birchwood seats in light yellow stain downstairs and slatted seats on the 'top deck'. I purposely say 'top deck' since it was named that and also because it could be like travelling on the top deck of a small coaster in a choppy sea. It was a copy of the Big Dipper in an amusement fair as swinging sideways, bounding and swaying up and down on miles of roads metalled in granite setts, while the wind and rain (in OUR tram there was no roof at all on the top deck) ruffled the hair and the water fell on the deck and drained away into the lee or starboard scuppers, accompanied by the screams and hum of the trolley pulley, with blinding and crackling flashes lighting up the roadside (especially after dark) between pulley and high-tension wire. With every bend or turn at speed the wheels, influenced by the road's camber, smote with their rims against the grooved rails and hummed and rang like chinese gongs. It sounds exciting: we thought it was, and all for one penny. At a crossroads or obstructing vehicle or anything similar that delayed progress the driver would clang his resonant deep-toned bell. Some driving cabs were even more primitive than ours and had no enclosing screen for the driver and there he stood in heavy black rainwear and flat uniform cap covered against wet with a mackintosh cover gathered with elastic, shod in heavy boots or wellingtons, and peering over the metal waist high surround centred by the headlight for hazards ahead. In fog he was quite dependent on the driver ahead since it was impossible for him to overtake, and huge traffic jams built up at an amazing speed. The conductor who accepted fares carried a variety of tickets of differing colours, uses and charges, which were printed in thin card, and ingeniously carried around clipped to a wood and metal frame and hanging from the left wrist by a leather strap. An issued ticket was musically punched like the bell on a typewriter by a cancelling machine, which the conductor carried with him.

There was another art-form besides films that one could indulge in free, and I certainly indulged: it was painting. A small, provincial art gallery housed in a medium-sized and classically designed country house and surrounded by almost a thousand acres of parkland lay one mile from where I lived. Admission was daily and free; consequently we went there often to watch and observe. Perhaps I was a little surprised that the late occupants – the house now belonged to Manchester city – had lived in such style and surroundings. Even the story of Cinderella had not prepared me for this, and the possibility of having spaciousness, quality and beauty around one instead of the cramped utilitarianism and basic shelter of an artisan's dwelling of two up and two down came as a mild shock. Entering the house multiple pairs of doors in figured Spanish mahogany with ormulu furniture and elaborate plaster jambs and architraves opening on most rooms drew my attention and admiration. A wide, shallowed stepped staircase rose from a marble-pillared hall; painted and gilded cast iron lamp posts elegantly mounted on tripods and surrounded with simple and tasteful glass lanterns caught my attention: how splendid to be thus lighted to bed instead of a naked batswing jet on a plain gas pipe, I decided, and on the floor lavishly polished wood. My lady's circular boudoir, surrounded by a dozen, spaced cheval glasses, was something to see again and again, but most of all I wanted the pictures. English watercolours, they drew me like a magnet more than anything else there.

   In time I learned to some degree to recognise the style of David Cox, some of whose paintings seemed, unlike most water colours, quite large. Only Samuel Prout appeared to turn out paintings of like size but Prout's paper was whiter and smoother – at times I was sure I could recognise tiny fragments of straw in the rough, grey or off-white paper Cox used. There were other differences too. Cox was a man of the wind and the rain, whether on the sea or, more commonly, in hilly country, often Wales, and the trees, the rocks, the sheep and the human figures knew the elements and lived in them. His subdued blues and sepias that enhanced the distances in his work were in marked contrast to the milder pastel shades of

Prout. Another thing, Prout used town scenes, and churches, ancient and historical buildings inhabited by many more humans with carts and coaches, 'diligences' they were called, moving in and out of the streets. His colours, like Copley Fielden's, had choice, wider and more liberal colour selection and his skies seemed set for fair weather. Fielden's were small pictures of meticulous draughtsmanship not a bit like David Cox's bustling with enormous energy. Fielden's were exquisitely tinted and more like Thomas Girtin's, though the latter artist used a more limited palette. Girtin's work pleased me immensely. There weren't enough of his to compare – and his method, especially in the painting of Furness Abbey, is now known as 'wet on wet', the paint being floated onto damp areas of paper. Others that appealed were Paul de Loutherbourg, Peter de Wint and the Varley brothers. Not all the pictures took my fancy: there was an oil by Turner which ran with colour. It seemed as if the artist had applied a fully loaded brush and, without brushing out the paint, left it to run down the canvas in thin runnels, nor had ever returned to the work. Other oil colours by John Linnell and by Richard Wilson I did like as well as a most realistic English country scene with cattle by William Shayer, but on the whole, probably because of their size, I was better able to enjoy the watercolours. No doubt, nowadays schoolchildren are regularly instructed in art in galleries and the things to look for and appreciate are fully explained, but I had to find my own way, limited though it was, and I am deeply grateful to the City Fathers there who allowed me the run of the place.

CHAPTER SEVENTEEN

Adventures in Irwell Vale

Here, ages ago, an ancient river flowed into a lake, and the rich deposited sediment it had brought now formed the level floor of the valley a mile wide and several miles long. Between that time and now the lake had disappeared and the river, still flowing, moved over to the right hand side above a fault in the strata, and through the long years had cut a sixty-foot ravine in the out-cropping rock. The valley width was the natural boundary between teeming town with its offensively noisy industry, sooty public buildings and seemingly endless rows of granite setts, and the rural parish adjoining, half buried in an undulating seclusion of fields, copses and little dells.

During the early railway age the iron way crept along valley sides parallel, sponsored by get-rich-quick promoters, but because of the geological fault only one stretch of line developed financially. This side passed pitheads and metal, coal and ceramic industries. The further side ran through quiet ways where the carboniferous strata lay too deep to exploit, and the land was extensively agricultural and thus its permanent way gathered and deposited little freight. Passengers also were few so that in time its five stations became two, mere halts embowered in greenery. Soon after the second halt the railway turned right wheel and joined the busier line by means of a great viaduct.

This viaduct built of blue engineering bricks thirteen arches long stretched across the valley floor at right angles to the river, crossing the stream in one effortless bound with a beautiful and larger seventh arch. The rocky banks on which the piers of this arch were placed furnished an anchor point for a stone abutment keyed into the living rock and projected into the stream like the salley of an ancient castle. The abutment deflected the scouring current, preventing the undermining of the pier on that side. Now the apex of the larger arch, that serene bow of many thousands of bricks, could not have been less than eighty feet above the water's surface, but higher still, rising above the parapet and its stone feather-edging, stood the signal box, at approximately mid-channel, with the signalman like a sea captain on a ship's bridge. Our walks to 'Thirteen Arches' took a day.

Along the ravine sides randomly planted stands of hardwood trees struggled to survive in polluted air blowing from the factories, and toxic sulphur dioxide fumes claimed victims yearly, yet still Nature asserted herself to restore the balance. Oaks, sycamore and beech trees, beneath whose boughs wild hyacinths bloomed in springtime, seemed from the distance to rise from rich blue-misty fields, so thickly grew the flowers, and as the tree buds unfolded each tree could be recognised according to its kind, by the shade of green. The oaks were a mustard green, the green of parched peas that have been boiled too long; the sycamores were darker with a splash of burnt umber, and besides, the tree disposed its leaves in tiers like the tiers of a grand wedding cake and could thus otherwise be recognised. The beeches were of a stronger, darker green and towered above the other trees. Beneath them the shadows were very deep.

A matter of a furlong upstream and parallel to the viaduct, but much inferior to it in size and height, indeed only a little higher than the ravine sides, stood an aqueduct of yellow stone, and from which, randomly chosen by wind and suitable matrix, grew hardy ferns, sprouting bright fronds in the summer months. The aqueduct carried a short section of one of the narrow broad canals that followed a low contour along the valley. From his elevated position the signalman could see that the permanent way he controlled was in plan a duplication of the navigation of half a century earlier, and the three factories accordingly took advantage of both facilities, each establishment having its railway siding and canal wharf.

Described in 1838 as 'a valley rich with the choicest beauties of rural scenery which could scarcely be surpassed . . .', a little later the district had a famous Society of Botanists, working men all, and a local inn named after the new railway and the naturalists, in that order.

This place was so far from our homes that we visited it only when we had a full day to spare and could bring with us our sandwiches and bottles of fizzy drinks. Common sense kept us a stone's throw from the industry, for it was a noisome place and besides, there was always a labourer to question our approach and to threaten us, even with the canal between.

By the ceramic wharf, from a six inch drain a continuous stretch of milkiness, diluted slip seeping into the canal, created a cloudy, opaque stream where nothing ever grew, yet the steady flood of water in turn dissipated the whiteness and only a short distance further on water plantain and flags reappeared.

The next factory was offensive to nose, ears and eyes: drifting veils of exhausted boiler steam floated from many traps and pipes and in the moister air the nose became more susceptible to the ever-present stench. Sprawling heaps of burning vulcanite waste gave off dense, greasy black smoke in contrast to which that smoke from the bottle kilns seemed less offensive. There was an acridity of chlorine and a real or imagined taste of metal on the lips as one has after handling much copper coinage. Ears were assailed with the hammering of power presses and the clang, screech and screaming whine of metal meeting metal.

Here we crossed the humpback bridge and so up the pathway of small cobbles where the tow horse changed from one side to the other. Guarding it stood a massive eight-foot restraining post where the rope friction of almost a century and a half had gouged deep parallel channels to half the post's girth. We trailed our hands over marble-smooth stone parapets bound with iron straps, and stared down into the deeps of the water, continuing for a further mile to a disused spur of the canal where a graveyard of narrow boats, hulk after hulk, lay fascinating, eerie and romantic.

Some boats showed only a prow and some a stern with or without a tiller and slanting heavy wooden rudder. Some showed all the upper work and some were still cargoed with empty coal tubs of robust timber construction, but each and every one holed below the water line. They bore no names – only the number the colliery had provided – while pond weed grew in them along with rushes and reed mace palisaded them round about. On the surface floated duckweed, a smothering blanket of minute, vivid green discs. Here in summer brilliant and bronzed demoiselles in blue and green darted and hovered above the gaudy flags with their strap-like leaves and ramrod stiffness, and in late August the golden, gauzy-winged great dragon fly alternately clung to the leaf and patrolled up and down his territorial stretch.

This spur of the navigation ended at a small tower of dark red brickwork badly in need of pointing, about ten feet high, and crowned with a high railing of sharp iron spikes deeply pitted with rust. Into the base of the tower as into a vast mouth the canal overflowed, and by way of a shallow stone sill and wooden hatch, smoothly slid through an arch, heavily barred. Unseen but heard the waters disappeared into this well with a thrilling roar while at one corner a wayward water jet, spraying sideways continuously, soaked the fleshy, green liverwort spreading over the masonry there.

'Never watch running water in the mass', we had been advised many times, 'unless there is a railing in front of you,' and so, fearfully turning away after the initial look, we moved away to other things.

Sooner or later we retraced our steps along the towing path, back over the yellow aqueduct and struck out across country to the quiet stretch of railway. Sometimes we followed field paths along the hedges bright in April, green leaf, disturbing unobtrusive dunnocks and chanting yellowhammers, while above us, the kestrels that nested in the put-log holes of the blue viaduct quartered the fields, hovering or gliding in short, rapid bursts of flight. A little earlier in the season it was the peewits who were most conspicuous in their fascinating behaviour. Over the meadows still bare after winter ploughing the sadly complaining birds on broad rounded wings flew erratically in mock attack, dropping vertically, wings like slowly turning sycamore keys falling from the sky, effortlessly checking the dive and lifting again vigorously or wheeling hither and thither in marvellous aerobatics. Sometimes we stumbled on their nests rather than found them, shallow saucers of soil with two or three large eggs like the brown eggs of a domestic fowl strikingly blotched in dark chocolate.

Our passage when May and early June had come was hazarded by sappy grass, long and wet with heavy dew or recent shower and we were soon wet in our boots, quicker still if we wore shoes, for socks soaked immediately even though we skirted the ditches fringed with horsetail and bedecked with water crowfoot and cuckoo flower. Accordingly we changed our route overland and persisted down the lane poorly metalled in crusted furnace clinker and grey, dusty coke ash.

Whitsuntide was well past but the prevailing colour of the wild flowers were white, and week after week white persisted. There was the light cream of cow parsley dominating the verges, umbels and finely fretted foliage nodding in the gentle wind, and backing it white mayblossom flowering to capacity on every quickthorn hedge or isolated tree. Elder flowers with flattened panicles coloured deep cream as cauliflower curds and heavily scented. In the hedge bottoms, garlic mustard still lingered with glowing metallic-white flowers as though made of an oxide of zinc. Here in the shadow of the wood could be detected a heavier, more pungent smell of garlic, the wild ramsons whose myriad heads as white as snowdrops stretched, thickly clustered, far away and out of view.

At the end of the lane at the further side of the valley an escarpment of pure sand rose above us, the existence of which we or any other passers-by might well be unaware but for the betrayal of its golden hillocks by the rabbits, for their burrows showed up like the bunkers of a golf course, and elsewhere was a thin black topburden covered with young woodland, or a scant outcrop of red sandstone poking through the acid soil.

Along the escarpment at a suitable contour the single rail track edged along for several miles through small stands of oak, birch and hazel and past a pine tree or two whose positions had been determined by chance rather than by choice. From mid April onwards the song of the willow tit and chiff chaff were heard above the soft chuff-chuffing of the locomotive and through the lush growth of the later season on sunny days the carriages were dappled in light and shadow, while through half-opened windows rich odours of bark and leaf and flower slowly distilling their sweetness in the humid alembic of high summer. The few travellers nodded and dozed in their pleasant indolence, overcome by the heat.

At the other side of the track along the course described lay a little dell, Fitch Holes, marked on the older maps but of such insignificance the railway builders threw a raised embankment at right angles to and across it, piercing the piled earth with a stone-faced culvert to allow natural springs and floodwater to drain away. Then they had forgotten it so that it remained secret and unknown to all but a few local folk. There were no paths there. Badgers had once occupied setts there, though not in living memory, but weasels could be seen, rarely, if one were fortunate to be there at the right time, and had a quick eye. Other small mammals roved its grassy floor, field mice commonly traversed it, and hedgehogs, and from time to time the body of the common shrew, that tiny animal with such an excitable temper and so many enemies, was found. This little area, difficult of access and hidden from many eyes, was our goal.

On once arriving we saw little cause to bustle along like the tiny brook sliding on its course along the valley floor, dropping in miniature cataracts over the sills and ledges of outcrop rock, or creeping under rank grasses or beneath the shadow of long bramble shoots where the half-buoyant water vole paddled, moving his blunt head from side to side searching for provender between the thick cresses. How pleasant it was to lie supine on sun warmed thymey turf below the heather bordering the valley side, and watch small copper butterflies busy on nettles and scabious heads and magenta thistles, the unheeded book (brought in the jacket pocket and meant to be read) lying open to the sky.

Thus the long summer passed. The bracken that had grown ever thicker and higher now lost its green resilience, stiffened with age and burned in the heat, but we had long returned to our classrooms before the heather flowers paled and the bramble fruits turned black. They, in turn, passed their peak of excellence as the blow flies sought them out, clinging, piercing and sucking until the fruits turned dull and unpleasant. Dog rosehips reddened and burnet rose hips became even more scarlet in the shrinking daylight hours of increasing coolness and brief evening gave place to night as the woodcock sought its roost among the hazel thicket and the owls began to call.

CHAPTER EIGHTEEN

Music, Mice & My Brother Charlie

I adored Charles, my big brother. He always had time for me, was gentle and protective especially at church concerts, classes and Sunday school parties when that hated game 'spinning the platter' always came. I accompanied him everywhere, on cycle rides to the River Irwell, on walks in Heaton Park where he showed me exotic fungus like 'stinkhorn' and how to plait grasses into whips at the 'rushy whip place'. As time went by, I

John Charles Houghton, artist and musician, Lake District, c. 1932.

accompanied him to St Margaret's Church and sat in the organ loft where I did my Latin homework and revision for exams while he practised for Sunday service and weddings. He once told me that among the organ voluntaries while waiting for a bride, who insisted on coming late, he played a piece he was unfamiliar with but suitably melodious. He later discovered, much to our amusement, that it was entitled 'Leave me, deceiver', but best of all he played at my wedding in 1950 when the vicar himself forgot to turn up.

There were few telephones in those days. Charles rapidly changed from 'Here comes the Bride' to – was it again 'Leave me, deceiver'? It took quite a time to winkle out that forgetful vicar and Charles's repertoire was again stretched. My attentions were centred on Father, about to explode into one of his grand scenes of 'righteous indignation'. He had a point, but on that momentous day of my life I did eventually 'get spliced'. The parson who did not get to the church on time looked shaken and penitent when one of the sidesmen eventually rounded him up.

Some years later, when Charles had become a head of music, he told me the following story:

I was off to play in a concert and helping a student with his double bass. 'Actually,' he said, 'a double bass isn't very heavy'. I accompanied Tim to make him feel less conspicuous, but that giant of a string family is not the sort of thing one carries around by day, and certainly cannot be tucked under the right arm like a violin case. I suppose these days the student of the double bass carries it on the roof of his nippy little car. Times have changed, but anyone who has travelled with an awkward burden on a bus will sympathise, knowing the difficulties and embarrassments.

After vicissitudes in plenty we arrived late at our recital hall, where a distracted conductor wiped his brow as he spotted us.

'Thank goodness you've come. We're ready to start. Have you got your music?' My companion the bass player closed his eyes and smote his brow.

'I knew there was something missing,' he muttered. 'I left it in Coll. Never mind, I'll play from memory.'

Word got around the performers of this minor misfortune and the leader, more anxious than usual, fluffed his entry. The strings sank dejectedly in sympathy. It was a poor start.

The star singer sighed in my ear. 'I think I've got one of those throats coming on. Have you a sweet I might have?' I shook my head. Spirits sank deeper. Dejection sank in as she coughed quietly and huskily, bending her head over her clenched hand. Suddenly her eyes strayed over the audience, then became fixed, her mouth relaxed and she was smiling merrily. Her mood changed so quickly that she was shaking with suppressed laughter, which she covered by making two nervous coughs.

'Look at that radiator.' I looked and saw the cause of her humour. The packed audience was almost completely composed of women; wives, mothers, elder sisters and aunts. Behind them all, squatting on hind legs, was an inquisitive mouse who moved his head as though listening with great attention to detail. The obvious question was what would happen if one of the audience sitting by the radiator turned round.

The choir soon realised the situation and their lightened spirits stimulated the instrumentalists. From then on we couldn't go wrong. The mouse disappeared in the manner of a newspaper critic before the final item of a concert and not one member of the audience had realised it was there.

It was a decade later before music, mouse and I were to meet again. I resided at one of the country cottages which, along with three larger dwellings and a few scattered farms formed the hamlet from which the congregation of the tiny parish church was drawn. Because I attended the service and was known to be a professional musician I became unofficial organist. Actually half the residents attended the church; the other half attended a nonconformist chapel, but once a year on successive Sundays the two congregations joined, to fill church and chapel in turn at the Harvest thanksgiving.

Haymaking at Hesketh Lane, Southport, 1909.

Enormous machines like Britannia, seen here in about 1950, helped with harvesting well into the twentieth century.

Impartially and with great care each building was festively dressed, and since this was a farming area nothing was stinted.

It was the turn of the chapel to take precedence and I sat on the organ bench listening to the address which had just began. In a clear voice a minister from the circuit gave force to his statements by the free use of gesture. It was an interesting address but a sudden diversion caused me to transfer my attention elsewhere. Against the end of the choir stalls, behind the pulpit and against my bench stood a sheaf of wheat, straight from the field. There, front paws grasping a grain of wheat, gnawing away rapidly was a mouse. He ate several grains then, perhaps feeling in need of spiritual food, remained, poised, front paws crossed, and appeared to be listening to the minister as one of the congregation. He sat there quietly until the address came to an end, and as the closing hymn was announced disappeared in a flash over the other side. The following Sunday as I sat at the church organ I saw the visitor a second time, oddly at the same time during the address. Or was it the same visitor? He looked the same to me with his beady eye winking alertly. He ran in little darts along the top of the organ curtain rail, down the curtain and instantly up a nearby sheaf of wheat. Was this, I wondered, a church mouse, poor and worthy of Christian charity, seeking it in his own domain, or a dissenting mouse who had joined with the other members of the congregation from the chapel over the lane? Was he, putting it simply, making full use of the advantages of an ecumenical church?

Like many time-worn expressions 'poor as a church mouse' rings hollow in my ears. Out there is a world of rich mousey experience and rich pickings too, especially at harvest time.

Among unforgettable adventures I had with Charles one might be called 'Locked in and Locked out'. Attending for organ practice on the first occasion the verger accidentally locked us in the church. On the second, we could not get in. The door was fast shut. As it was more than a mile away from our home we did not want to give up. We got in and out via the coke chute, coke being used for central heating in those days, mountains of it. We became very dusty and black but inconspicuous as wartime blackout prevailed! When we reached home, the parents were dumbfounded at our appearance. We discovered that climbing up coke was harder than climbing down. I supposed it was quite dangerous.

That was not the only time in my youth that I came back black. My friend and I were invited to join a roller skating party. Not knowing exactly where we were being taken, I remember we travelled by tram (again it was in blackout wartime), ended up in Gorton in somewhat sleazy surroundings and arrived home very dishevelled and dirty. That occasion was even more dangerous because shortly afterwards the premises were flattened with German incendiary bombs during the Manchester Blitz, days before Christmas. Poor parents! What with that and a rock climbing brother, not to mention a coke climbing brother, we four siblings gave them some shocks.

CHAPTER NINETEEN

Trouble at th' Mills

The transition from childhood fascination to the harsh reality of life emerges when Charles starts work. I have left this account exactly as Charles wrote it.

Kearsley's mill lodge took the waters of the short, precipitous stream, and this stream, fed by several springs and field drains had its main source in a gentle hillside, and forming a narrow defile or clough, descended to the river meadows before falling into the main channel below. In the stream's higher reaches, where a child could stand astride its waters, the water mints grew thick, and buttercups could always be found. Later these plants gave way to wild garlic and meadowsweet, celandine, and higher up, wood anemone and oxalis. A colony of Indian balsam had climbed from the river verge and moved upstream also, but owing to the exceeding wetness of the site had taken no great hold thereon. Willows grew here in variety, and several alders. A wide meander, a low bank of golden sand where the undermined roots of birth trees entangled themselves and held back any immediate plant growth, was a favourite sunning place for passing butterflies; dragonflies, too, patrolled this spot in August. Behind the bank of a stream of iron water, deep orange, seeped from the ground and caused the grass to grow greener here than anywhere else. In time the clough opened out and the fall of water grew less boisterous, and channelled in gracious curves, moved on to the river, yet there was no dalliance to its flow, and the hot sunshine dimpled and glanced on its surface. There were banks of pebbles here from which the imprisoning boulder clay had long since been washed away, and here showed a glimpse of the underlying out-crop of new red sandstone. Here where the humble bees zoomed in May grew the pink flowers of butterbur, for the land was better drained, and plants from the stream's higher reaches were no longer found. A small patch of gorse or a broom or two flowered fitfully through the four seasons and here grew the oak and there stood the beech in fully glory.

A hardwood dam athwart the stream lay channelling most of its waters into a large mill lodge, puddled well with clay and buttressed with old railway sleepers and lengths of old steel rails, the whole buried under a wide bank of enclosing earth and masonry. This was the plentiful soft water without which the bleaching and dyeing industry could never have taken place.

Class V. A.H. at Stand Grammar School, Whitefield, 1938. We were told that Clive of India attended our school. Among the back row are Annie Ralphson, Josie Ogden, Margery Buchanan, Helen Nuttall and Vivian Sampson. In the front row are Edna 'Muffin' Smith, Catherine Houghton, Miss Edith Hargreaves, Jacqueline Colbert, Pauline Sampson, Eileen Freedman and Muriel Hadfield.

Up to the mid-eighteenth century the bleaching of linen, later cotton, was a lengthy business. After steeping the cloth in an akaline solution for several days (bucking) it was passed through rinsing water and exposed to the sun and elements in grassy meadows (crofting). This process was repeated several times, the whole action taking between six and eight months to complete. Whitefield where I attended grammar school is a place name that reveals its origins. Since we seem to have had light- fingered people always with us it will be understood that the safety of the cloth was under a continual hazard, and croft breaking was common though the penalty of being caught was death, one of the 220-odd offences to which the death penalty was attached in this country in those days. The last man who suffered this fate seems to have been George Russell who in 1798 was hanged on a gibbet in Newton Heath, for breaking into Mr Shorrock's croft. Towards the end of the century a new bleach of chlorine and lime began to be used, cutting down the time needed to complete the process, from months to days.

The bank had a road of river stones running alongside it and so well had this road been laid, keyed in some cunning way by a master hand, that it was quite impossible to pick out one single pebble without first shattering one. Years and years of wear, of human feet in clattering clogs and of the high-ringing rattle of the iron tyres of horse drawn drays had failed to make any rut or channel in the resistant surface. The sad, pitiful imitation

One of the mill girls at a cotton spinning loom, Enfield Mill, Wigan.

of these modern times, stones set upright in concrete, seems more like a miniature tank trap set to tear off the slender heels of young ladies' shoes, the higher the more hazardous, and deadly for anyone on foot when the pebbles have a coating of black ice, is reminiscent rather of blanched almonds stuck in marzipan by a tyro cook.

And so this broad road ran between the water and the mill buildings, bordered by gritstone kerbs set deep into the earth.

The buildings were old: three storeys high, brick built and having windows of many-paned glass, each floor above the ground being supported on cast iron pillars bearing square section wooden beams upon which the smaller, oblong joists rested. Years of steady maintenance in the days of plenty had preserved the fabric wonderfully well on the whole. Applications of pitch, coat upon coat, covered the mild steel railings surrounding the walls so that, beneath, they were as newly erected. A wooden bell tower fitted with louvres but from which the bell had long since been removed, stood above the roof, also pitch black, though its pyramidal apex where the droppings of so many birds showed white offered stark contrast. Limewash had been freely used in the interior. What artificial lighting had originally been used it was hard to conjecture, but a primitive system of electric cables borne upon white porcelain insulators ran the wall perimeter.

Two casualties of neglect, a pair of ancient keirs, vertical cylindrical tanks, solidly constructed of rivetted boiler plates, stood side by side, thick laminates of rust peeling from them.

The pointed railings which kept us away from the keirs lapped the buildings on three sides, but on the third section they entered the main wall by the bleaching shed, and with a chained gate which guarded the fixed bridge of railway sleepers, denying entrance to the stranger.

Down in the yard stood carboys of corrosive chemicals, the freshness or otherwise of the straw packing showing the time that had elapsed since they had been left there, and beside them, a dozen or so fifty gallon steel drums, supine and full or upright and empty.

During those hot, endless August afternoons in the summer school holiday as daily we stripped the white convolvulus flowers off the railings, swallows rested momentarily above us then swept off, cleaving paths across the cool running water, and jackdaws crying, wheeled and tumbled in the air. As the hours passed swifts began to ascend, screaming and rising in vast circles until lost to sight.

As day followed day the rosebay willowherb lifted higher than the surrounding grasses. Its paleness slowly changed to pink, then to mid magenta. Earth dried in the golden hours of sunlight and in advancing heat zephyrs sprang up and raised tiny dust whirls. Small copper butterflies fluttered above the flowering thistles; common browns patrolled the verges.

At times a door stood open and there was a glimpse of shafting and driving belts, and a skip or two on a loading bay, holding grey cloth, but seldom did anyone come to bustle about the area. On other occasions a labourer in brat (apron) and cloth cap and with shirt sleeves rolled to his elbows passed through the yard on some errand or other, or bearing on his shoulder a bolt of cloth. We could see and hear work going on in the building but never did anyone come and ask us why we lingered or sent us about our business.

And so the years passed slowly, and change itself was correspondingly slow and scarcely to be noticed, but change there was. The loaded drays became less frequently employed and the loads themselves diminished so that the green tarpaulins sagged hollow-cheeked over the dray centre bar. The sounds of industry grew less and at times the shafting was not moving, but an open window showed that there was life still inside. Labour no longer came to clean the windows, those many sparkling panes, and cobwebs, picked out in cotton lint dust increased in thickness, and flies, moths and an odd unfortunate wasp hung there in gossamer chains, pulsating in the wind, and thicker and yet more thicker grew the webs inside. Birds with increasing temerity nested over the dyehouse clerestories: if a slate slid off the roof it was no longer replaced. The loading bay remained unswept and oats dropped from the nosebag of the solitary dray horse blown by winds into some favourable seeding place, took root, flourished and bore harvest in the cracks and fissures of the way.

Kearsley's was at least a mile away from the village, at the end of a long, winding country lane, passing a country house, or a few cottages and a large farm if one kept religiously to the path. One could see the mill buildings in the shallow valley about a couple of furlongs before reaching it and here the lane forked, continuing to the mill but taking the right fork if one wished to end up at a rival establishment, well, hardly rival since it was so much more bustling, modern, efficient and of course, larger. This rival was Dewhurst's, and Dewhurst's bore as much relationship to Kearsley's as a modern hypermarket bears to an old-fashioned grocer's with the owner-assistant behind the counter in a large white apron and a personal approach.

Dewhurst's catchment area for their water supply sprang from the base of an escarpment of almost pure sand overlaid with boulder clay, the bank or raised terrace of the original river course and now a quarter mile from the river and running parallel with it for several miles. This was another favourite playground, for the steam provided us with minnows, and we wandered along its meanders under the oaks and beeches, and through the dark, glossy green grasses – called sheep's fescue tussocks – the tips of each clump, a mass of hair-like grass blades, turned brown in autumn, and they yielded long flowering 'silver spoons' valued by girls when out collecting wild flowers for home. Bordered yellow underwing moths were common here, and occasionally a weak-winged cinnabar moth in early September. I have seen shrews among this grass though I had not yet found a nest other than a warbler's nest. Where the grass thinned the 'sourdabs', our name for sorrel, spread, together with tormentil, in the impoverished soil. There was an approach for pedestrians only fenced by beech boughs, split lengthways with steel wedges and raised on square cut oak posts, and since there was no transport to either mill except one's own bicycle, very few of the staff owned cars, this path was the one generally favoured by workers.

On terminating my school life one Friday afternoon in July, the following day I was offered my first job at Dewhurst's. I learned something about its history then. Founded about the time of the First World War, probably dyeing khaki cloth, the place had steadily extended by using modern techniques and up-to-date machinery, and increasing the variety of cloth treatments, especially to supply the feminine demand for man-made fibres textiles. The place would have gone on from strength to strength but for one thing: the draught of the 1930s economic blizzard had already begun to strike rigid many of the older industries on which the prosperity of the nation depended. Some, of course, never woke from this icy sleep of death: cotton was feeling the cold strongly and India was turning out miles of her own textiles for home consumption. Every Monday morning one could see the effects of trade recession in the queue of unemployed labourers lined up outside the general office, hoping, and a slim hope it was, of being engaged. It could be seen in the works itself, in the silent bleaching sheds every Monday and Tuesday, for only on the next three days of the week did the place become alive; there wasn't enough work to last the whole week.

By seven every morning I signed on the office staff book by which time the labouring staff had been at their tasks an hour. At eight the stridency of the steam whistle brought a temporary stop to work and ushered in breakfast for the next thirty minutes, ten of which were wasted because of the poor facilities for providing drink; one had to queue up and there were but two lanes of workers. At that identical hour the Chairman of the company rang through to the office. I had to receive the call, for some person I knew not but who was somewhere in that complex of buildings. It could be a wild goose chase, and it often was. Punctually an hour later, coinciding with the arrival of the typists arrived also the Chairman. As this was my first essay into real work I found that I was feeling rather jaded by four-thirty in the afternoon when the typists drank their afternoon tea – there was none for the clerks – and if, after the hooter had sounded 'down tools' and I still had to wait upon the Chairman at his private residence two miles away – get there under my own steam, and wait until he signed the mail, I would arrive home about the time I should have been beginning my first Commercial class at night school. That time was seven-thirty, and I had still to eat my evening meal, the first food since twelve-thirty. As I sat in his kitchen, empty as the proverbial drum, a cook would open the Esse oven and take out a large roasting tin in order to baste the capon it contained. I won't pursue the trend of thought I held then, I'm sure that you can easily guess. I should also point out that I occupied that job for six months before I was allotted a chair. It was probably assumed, and quite truthfully in fact, that I would be too much occupied with important matters pertaining to my place of employment than to allow my mind to stray on to the fleshy temptation of sitting and giving my legs a rest. Unused to such treatment I soon developed the painful symptoms of foot stress, fallen arches. Beyond provoking ribaldry from some quarters I was given no sympathy, not even by my doctor who merely questioned my lack of stamina, and that was all. At work I gathered brickbats, never bouquets, but that seemed to be the lot of the office drudge in those wretched days.

Several times a day I moved round the buildings distributing or collecting cyclostyled sheets pertaining to each order and the processes demanded for the same. From bleach house to merceriser; grey room to singe house; stenter one to stenter two and on to direct dye, vat dye and fancy dye with their rows of triangular steel troughs and vast vat where man-made textile fabrics tumbled in steaming troughs of solutions and so on to white collander sheds one and two and on to finishing room and make-up rooms until I knew each cloth process from memory. To see an endless, wet, twisted rope of cloth hurtling at so many miles per hour through a series of porcelain eyes from room to room and fed into the insatiable maw of vertical or horizontal keir was exhilarating, and the smells there added to that infection: the unpleasantness of chlorine in the bleach house mingling with the vinegary draughts from next door, the merceriser, and oh, the sweatiness in the stenter!

The directors were related to each other, all members of one family, father, sons, cousins, uncle and alas, I seemed to rattle the lot. Pity I pray, pity for gauche youth fallen among you! I jostled the elder son in passing him (he was twice as big as I was and furthermore had a director's backside); I kept the younger son, Master Cedric, waiting, WAITING on the 'phone far too long when searching for him, for a man who was off work ill. I gave the answers to the Chairman's enquiries in a way he considered unsuitable. They were straight and direct, though never impertinent, but they were not tempered with the right amoung of smooth approach, of studied deference as befitted one in my humble station. Worst of all I kept uncle waiting, for his tea, and that was unforgivable. Actually I was detained in the making-up room waiting for an urgent order to be made ready for the Chairman, but I should have got the tea before going. It was no use saying that on principle he refused his tea before the time indicated. Basically I had to be taught the 'right attitude' to my employer, and that was enough. The employer's decision was final, in those days. Uncle was put out; Uncle was cross; Uncle threatened to fire me there and then, but he slowly relented, or rather, it occurred to him he hadn't asked the Chairman's approval first. But . . . but, if it happened again . . .! It didn't happen again, for within the week Uncle had left us for other spheres. He suddenly died.

I had feared that I would get into his bad books again but there was no need to worry; my fate at this establishment had already been decided. Of course, I had to go, and before I was sixteen and thus liable for an Insurance stamp, and a minimal rise in salary, and I was dismissed without notice while the job passed to a fourteen year old boy whose father habitually supported the bar in the Chairman's club. The letter of dismissal arrived on Good Friday (yes, post was delivered on that day then) and I was so stunned I stayed away from church, or perhaps was taken on a picnic to help me forget. I was such an innocent that I believed I had failed to hold down a job, the inadmissible fault among the hard-working artisan class. It was so difficult to find a job at that time that to lose one's employment was tantamount to a dereliction of duty.

During this initial job I began to be aware of the pettiness of the adult mind and the animosity, even to the point of frightening malevolence that seemed to, as it were, exude from one or two older people. Adults, it appeared to me had a built-in dislike of many of their fellow humans, and their peevishness could be every bit as great as that of a child, and last far, far longer. A postman, by mistake, had brought to the works a small bottle of dye that was addressed to Kearsley's. The secretary passed it to me and directed that it should be returned to the post office. Yet when I innocently suggested that it would be easier and more helpful if I took it across to the other place on my way home I was answered with a frown and, 'You will do as you are told, and on no account will you deliver it to the other place', almost as though I had suggested something most reprehensible like compounding a felony.

And so I left for good my first place of employment on Maundy Thursday, and for forty years I never set foot near the place, then by chance finding myself on my native heath again – it was again Good Friday – I paced the old road.

Along the clough and towards the river I trod, and at first it seemed that little had changed; the old vistas were still recognisable. There was Kearsley's, looking a little older, and a few things were missing, but substantially the same. It was still in use though not for dyeing and bleaching. I turned towards the river, and there was Dewhurst's, and though all the buildings semed to be there the place was dead; all was locked and barred, and had been for many a long year. 'Oh, that place?' said a passer-by, 'it's a warehouse or depository of sorts: it was a busy works in the old days, but that was long before my time.'

I smiled and thought a little, and then turned my back to it.

CHAPTER TWENTY

Manchester Memories

From my birthplace in an area of Lancashire once known as Oldham-with-Prestwich the nearest city, Manchester, seemed to exercise the greatest influence over the whole of Lancashire, overshadowing the county town of Lancaster, though both were soused in history, dating back further than the Romans. Wherever you looked, whatever you wanted, Manchester could supply. It was a power house, with its Cathedral; Free Trade Hall, new white Central Library resembling London's Albert Hall; Victoria University, once Owen's College; Alfred Waterhouse's Town Hall; St Ann's Church; Halle Orchestra; art galleries, cinemas and theatres where shows were staged before opening in London. It was often said that 'what Manchester thinks today, the world thinks tomorrow'. Indeed it seemed that Samuel Johnson's comment on London could have been applied appropriately to Manchester: 'The man who is tired of Manchester is tired of life'.

It was just before Christmas 1940 when the night sky was ablaze with incendiary bombs. Dawn revealed a city in ruins. In the dreary months

London Road station, Manchester, 1910.

The Shambles in Manchester, a place of great antiquity near the cathedral. All this disappeared on 23 December 1940, the night of the Manchester Blitz. I remember seeing Manchester burning from our house in Heaton Park, 5 miles away.

which followed when snow and debris littered the streets, great artists like Kathleen Ferrier and Isobel Baillie had to perform Handel's *Messiah* at Belle Vue, home of prize fights, while foreign films were shown in 'flea pits'. Everyone had his or her own particular and peculiar memories of the blitz. My father mourned for a favourite horse stabled at the old Flat Iron Market and the loss of Billy Dragg's scrap yard where he had spent many happy hours. With my brother who was home on leave I remember going to Manchester to watch ballet, which included Mussorgsky's 'Night on a Bare Mountain'. In the midst of that performance there was an air raid. It was at that historic time of the Second World War that the Siege of Stalingrad was raging: the name 'Stalingrad' was on every lip.

So many beautiful, spacious buildings were shattered by the blitz, yet as whole areas were cleared and the shells of buildings peeled away, interesting history was revealed, of which Manchester had plenty. It was not until the city was brought to its knees that local historians seemed to concentrate more on its past. The past is inseparably interwoven with the present and provides a pointer for the future. My childhood Manchester is as a palimpsest upon which streets and buildings were written, erased and re-written, so that to return would evoke memories rushing out like urchins screaming for attention: the wonder of seeing Peter Pan flying above the stage at the Princes Theatre; talking to the Indian 'Grey Owl' at the Free Trade Hall; climbing rickety stairs to antique shops in the

Shambles; the renowned jazz guitarist Django Reinhardt visiting our house for tea between sessions at Mamelok's on Oxford Road. Above all – student days 'When all the world was young, lad, And all the trees were green, And every goose a swan, lad, And every lass a queen.'

The rivers Irwell and Irk evoke a scene of murky waterways in which to fall would be a fate worse than death, yet 200 years ago they were clear enough for eels to flourish and in the fifteenth century fishing rights were rented to secure fish for the clergy during Lent. Records kept since 1616 reveal floods which drowned men, horses, sheep and pigs. One notable 'very high flood' in December 1837 tells of 'water in New Bailey Street and Broughton Road, with cattle, furniture and a baby in a cradle floating down the river'.

The New Bailey had replaced the dreaded Fleet, but was still fearfully referred to as 'The Dungeon' or 'The House of Correction' and was visited by penal reformer John Howard. The keeper, a chandler who kept inmates busy spinning candlewick at one penny ha'penny a pound, had just enjoyed a salary increase from £25 to £60. Living at Strangeways Hall, later the site of another prison, was Colonel Hanson who campaigned for higher wages to be paid to weavers. Manchester Authorities responded by fining him £100 and sentencing him to six months' imprisonment which damaged his health to such an extent that he died two years later at the age of 37. Shortly after his release from Lancaster prison, 32,000 grateful weavers subscribed one penny each to present him with a gold cup.

It is astonishing that in that area were several ponds in which Mancunians swam and skated on during frosty weather, although, sadly, a number fell through the ice, including a well-known muffin-crier. Wherever you look in Manchester you find history writ in names, some going back to the Roman station at Knott Mill and to medieval times. The foundations of a Roman fort wall were found at Castle Field near the confluence of rivers Medlock and Irwell. Where the Old Apple Market used to be was the inn of that name which had a beautiful painted inn sign of an apple tree 'in full fig'. As early as 1596 a house in Mill Gate (Mylngate) had a common oven, which led to the name Bakehouse Court, still there in the 1970s. Balloon Street was so named because a Mr Sadler ascended twice from this spot in the first English balloon in about 1785.

The annual Lancashire rush-bearing ceremony led to an interesting sketch by artist Alexander Wilson who lived by Howarth's Gates in Long Mylngate, the Howarths being an influential local family. Apart from the ceremony itself in which the rush-cart was dragged from Piccadilly Flags, the sketch showed Manchester men of the day: 'Gentleman Cooper' who walked every year to Doncaster and back to watch the St Leger race; Henry Slater, innkeeper of the Bay Horse Tavern. Set amid fields and orchards in the Balloon Street area, the Howarth's mansion was later used as a tavern, 'The Manchester Arms'.

Among many inns of great antiquity one of the oldest was 'The Sun Inn and Poets' Corner'. From being 'well conducted' and of some literary tone it

The Bull's Head, Manchester, thought to be the city's oldest inn. On the night the city was visited by the Luftwaffe Ye Olde Wellington Inn, built in the fifteenth century, was left standing in the midst of the ruins.

became so infamous that its licence was taken away. The Bull's Head was where questions affecting the town were discussed. Earlier it was the headquarters of Prince Charles' army.

Only a street away from here was Chetham's Hospital amid warehouses, factories and shops. The 'spacious and antique mansion with low-browed roofs and narrow windows' sojourns on to this day, devoted to music. To visit its wonderful library is like stepping back in time. Entered from a quiet courtyard, the lofty, timbered hall conjures up medieval banquets accompanied by the lute and madrigal. Hundreds of years ago the space between Bridge Street and Jackson's Row was taken up by Blenorcard, a wilderness of trees. Through this overgrown area threaded the ancient Dene Gate, derived from Danes' Gate. Gradually the trees were felled and by 1711 it had become The Ridge, a pleasant place of meadows and cherry gardens.

As Manchester's industries flourished the singer and composer Richard Baines wrote a popular ballad which was hummed in the streets:

. . . 'Manchester's improving daily, the plough and harrow are now forgot, 'Tis coals and cotton boil the pot' . . .

SALFORD WAKE

Will be held as usual on MONDAY and TUESDAY, the 30th and 31st August, 1819, with

EVERY AMUSEMENT

In the Old English Style.

MONDAY, a *Jack Ass Race* for a Purse of Gold, to be rode in true Jockey Style—no crossing nor jostling to be allowed.

N. B.   There will be plenty of Bread and Cheese and strong Ale for those who bring Asses to Enter.   No less than three to start except by permission of the Steward.

A *Foot Race* of a Mile for a good HAT, by Men of all Ages, 3 to start or no race.

LOTS of RIBBONS to be Danced for by *Old Maids* and *Young Men.*

A *Young Pig* will be turned out with its Ears and Tail Soaped or Greased, and the person who catches it first and holds it by either, will be declared entitled to it.

Grinning through a Horse Collar by Boys under 18; the best to have Five Shillings.   3 to start or no Race.

TUESDAY, A *Grand Smoking Match* by Gentlemen of all ages, for a Pound of Bagshaw's Tobacco.

Thick Porridge Eating by Boys under 18, the best to have five shillings—the second, three shillings—and the third one shilling—Six to start or no porridge.

A *Sack Race* for a good Hat—the second to have half a Gallon of Ale.   Three to start or no race, without permission of the Steward.

A *Good Hat* to be run for by *Wooden Legged Men* of all ages.   Three to start or no race.

A *Grand Wheelbarrow Race*, the best of heats for a Purse of Gold—the second best to be entitled to five shillings.

N. B.   To prevent accidents, the Wheelbarrows will be inspected previous to the race by a person properly qualified.

If any disputes should occur, they will be decided by the Steward or whom he shall appoint.

W. CLAYTON, ESQ. STEWARD.

N. B. *The Amusements to commence precisely at Two o'clock each day.*

A poster advertising Salford Wake, 1819.

The last bull-baiting was held at Red Bank. This cruel 'sport' had been a popular feature of the Annual Wakes Meetings, whose programme also included sack race, smock-steeple chase, bolting hot porridge, swarming up the greasy pole and 'the genuine Tim Bobbin feat of grinning through a horse collar' . . . John Fletcher, who died in 1785, had an iron foundry at Red Bank and the Wakes presented opportunities for his brawny workforce to show off their stamina.

Wealthy linen draper John Quincey leased a long-gardened burgage plot in the 'Parsonage Lands' off what is now Deansgate. He was uncle to the famous Thomas de Quincey, the 'English opium eater' and his residence, where Thomas was born, was bounded by the narrow passage Black Fryars, 'with free liberty or way to the spring or well called Parsonage Well'. Thomas de Quincey's father built a house at Greenhay, away from the city, but as Manchester spread, this house became part of an ever-widening conurbation. Contrast this with the days of King Charles I when 'the royal borough could only boast two streets, all else being green fields and pasture with here and there a solitary homestead'.

In the chasing of Father Time through Manchester's history we are reminded that this great city is again moving centre-stage, preparing for the rest of the world to sit up and take notice.

CHAPTER TWENTY-ONE
Music Hath Charms
& Curtain Up

We came from a music-loving family. Great Grandfather Houghton queued a great length of time and at high cost to hear Jenny Lind sing, though he had never learned to play a musical instrument beyond a rough and ready rendering with two fingers in the right hand and basic chords in the left. He had, and so had Father, a bursting budget of songs of every description that we learned from memory by his singing. Some were very revealing of the type of song taught in the elementary schools established under the Compulsory Education of Forster's Act of 1870. 'Murmur gentle lyre' moved to a song of cricket and a setting of Felicia Hemans: 'Trembling now the lily weeps, faded the roses shiver.' There were reminders of Charles Lamb, Blake and Kingsley and their concern for boy chimney sweeps:

> Sweep, sweep cries little Jack
> With brush and bag upon his back.
> . . . He once was pretty Jack
> And had a kind mama . . .
> But foolish child he ran away . . .

'What was Mama doing to allow such a state of affairs?' I reasoned, while our flaxen-haired toddler, who understood the song perfectly well, cried her eyes out. However, that did not stop Father from doing it again. Many of Father's songs were harrowing but 'My Grandfather's Clock', I have learned since, was even popular in the United States. It was taught to the children of Bethesda Street, Burnley, a century ago and the headmaster recorded in his log book that the children sang it with enthusiasm.

This spate of music could not fail to have effect. Charlie joined the Anglican choir and learned to play the piano. Vaughan Williams was Music Editor of the *English Hymnal*, the book which he used, and with this and the *Cathedral Psalter* he learned to point the psalms, getting a good basic training which led eventually to the post of Head of Music and church organist.

A brass band at Poulton Gala in 2005. In the background is the Thatched House.
The first Thatched House Tavern had a thatched roof and adjoined the churchyard.
They had a brewhouse for making ale and the innkeeper was Nathaniel Charnock.

Charlie's piano was not a new one although a later model than those with fret-work fronts, scarlet ruched silk backings and candelabra. Called a cottage piano and having a wooden frame, its tone was delicate and hesitant on some keys as one might expect from a genteel old lady in figured walnut who had known better times. It suffered also from piano arthritis. Several of its jacks would, at moments of stress, totter from their upper parts and cause the hammers to fall back on their strings. To prevent this movement strips of pink sticking plaster were affixed to the damaged members, rendering touch a little uneven, but sound was still there. I distinctly remember a man with horse and cart taking it away, my parents having sold it for three pounds when, for Charlie's benefit, we graduated to a German overstrung which weighed a ton. There was also a revolving piano stool which stood in for merry-go-round when inspiration flagged. We children whirled round upon it in turns in an ecstasy of revolutions which brought on dizzy 'dos'.

The toy that Charlie had loved most was a cheap tin musical box emitting four faint notes, a theme of many possibilities, germ of melodies

Granny Brown, who was famous for her braised ox tongue (a recipe I still have to this day). Here she poses proudly with her grandsons Eddie (on lap) and Ernest. She lived at Lostock Hall near Preston and was married to a gamekeeper on the Worden Hall estate.

yet unheard. Perhaps it set him off in his exploration of music. As he sat quietly turning the handle and listening did he hear 'the horns of Elfland faintly blowing?' Certainly it was on Christmas Eve that through the crisp night air we both heard a ravishing sound. The Congregational Chapel Choir annually borrowed a wooden motor pantechnicon and using its natural resonance for their singing and for shelter when the weather was bad, toured the parish, rendering Christmas carols. This competent choir awakened us to the seasonal hymn 'Christians awake, salute the happy morn.' The amazing sweetness and wonder of this moment was akin, years later, to the seconds after my daughter was born in a Catholic nursing home. As I was wheeled towards the ward, 'Hail Marys' cadenced echoingly.

What I know of the real McCoy theatre, until recently, I thought, came from my stage-struck father and grandfather. By the time this interest rubbed off on me, black and white silent films, soon to be followed by 'the talkies', had arrived, causing some young women to feel emancipated if they smoked 'Casket' cigarettes, 'delightful to inhale, threepence a packet'. For me, emancipation meant visiting the 'flea pit'. I'm quite sure about the fleas for I found one snugged down in the sleeve of my jumper after *Les Enfants du Paradis*. Theatre management did its best, sluicing down pink marble corridors resembling brawn, with Jeyes Fluid seven days a week, the fumes from which fought desperately with the reek of tobacco smoke, but this did not deter; nor did the long ride by bus on what always seemed a wet, greasy afternoon.

Once in my worn, red plush, tip-up seat, raptly following the black and white flicker of wicked Ambrose persecuting medieval witches, or Arletty and Jean-Louis Barrault adorning sets reminiscent of Impressionist paintings, I was lost to the world. Father had been hopelessly stage and cinema struck, but Mother's side were Wesleyan Methodists, denied drinking, dancing and theatre, so it was against fearful odds, which in early years involved diligent if furtive recovery of pop bottle deposits that I scraped together ninepence of two and sixpence to see Robert Donat in *The Doctor's Dilemma* and Olivier and Richardson in *The Government Inspector*. Fifty years on, that seemed a bargain, especially with names like Fonteyn,

This photograph from 19 August 1950 was taken by my father's friend Carl Cloud, who had a photographic studio in Oxford Street, Manchester. A generous man, he brightened father's life at Christmas. His heavy equipment was kept in good repair by my father who was particularly skilled at mending the leather bellows on old-fashioned cameras.

Helpman and Gielgud and such plays as *Ghosts, Precious Bane, Candida, Mrs Warren's Profession, Lady Windermere's Fan*; such companies as D'Oyley Carte, Covent Garden, Royal Carl Rosa and the Old Vic.

Thoughts slide to fifty years ago. Treading the dusty boards of an attic, surrounded by shabby Victorian bric-a-brac and the detritus of a century brought back memories like a throng of unruly children screaming for attention. I had thought the attics of Britain swept clean by demands from charity shops, car boot and jumble sales, but here lay one subject to no wind of change. Here had lived a distant relative close to my heart, a fact made obvious by cogent evidence.

Passing over feathered boas, antimacassars and lurching bamboo plant stands, I delved into the paper work. There were old Christmas cards of great charm, visiting and birthday cards expressing the gentle humour of a pre-war era, but most interesting of all were the masses of theatre programmes from which leapt great names and record performances: Enrico Caruso; Madame Patti; Martin Harvey; Clara Butt; Harcourt Beattie; Ronald Bayne; Mrs General Tom Thumb and the American Lilliputian Company – even pantomime, complete with 'every child's dream', the Transformation Scene. My ears filled with the thunder of clapping hands, as in mind's eye, lit by limelight, rich-red velvet curtains braided with heavy gold, rose and fell like yo-yos.

Small advertisements alongside the evening's entertainment added further interest, not to mention commanding documentation: 'Consult Madame Blanche, corset specialist, for unbreakable Empirella steels;' 'Wear Dunn's famous hats'; 'Do not be without Veldtic Boots', but a glowering hint of things to come cropped up in the most sensational play of the year: 'Monday 21 March 1921, *The Right to Strike*.'

Out of this cornucopia there fell a solitary dance programme, deckle-edged, with its slim, white pencil dangling. The date was arresting: 24 November, my birthday, but the year was 1899. Twenty dances with French-sounding titles were printed in two neat columns, but the pristine pasteboard was devoid of partners' names. Perhaps it was years later that my ancestor wrote on the back: 'I did not learn to dance.' The same hand informed her parents when she left Lytham for Goodson's drapers in Deansgate, Manchester: 'I knew everything at the shop on the first day so I am not too tired but we do not close until 9 o'clock at night.' With infectious enthusiasm she also wrote to a soldier friend, Arthur, about Mrs Patrick Campbell: 'Have you seen her? she was born in 1855 and was the first Eliza Dolittle.'

Ethel, I mused, must have been my father's age, but whereas he loved the friendly, boisterous atmosphere of the Alexandra Music Hall, later the 'Tiv' or Tivoli Theatre, and such spectacular occasions as The Wild West Coming to Town, she gloried in plays and opera. To the Royalty Theatre and Opera House came Gilbert and Sullivan when the D'Oyley Carte in their tour northwards stopped off in 1899. In contrast, when Buffalo Bill's Circus came to the Hippodrome on 21 September 1904, Colonel Cody brought

Sir George Robey
(1869–1954), English
comedian. He lived near
my uncle William in
Herne Hill.

500 horses, choking the area with people, wagonnettes, laudaus and horse-drawn trams.

To the intrepid Ethel, devotee of 'Curtain Up', distance was no object. In her ankle-length, blue, Devon serge skirt she sped by train or horse bus, after a working week of sixty hours, to see Henry Irving in *The Bells* or the fabled Miss Fortescue in *Moths*. No time for dancing! Ever-changing theatre was her glamorous escape route. The programme bore witness, notes in the margins widening her admiration and enjoyment.

Dust motes swarmed in a sudden gleam of sunshine brightening the grimy fanlight. It was high time to leave the attic which I had entered as a stranger but where I had found a friend. Across the gulf of a century I saluted this stage-struck lass, distant blood-sister of mine. 'Oranges, cakes, sweets, programmes, a penny each!' 'The play's the thing!' Was that an echo down the years? No doubt about it; the lure of the footlights was in the family genes.

CHAPTER TWENTY-TWO

Don't Shoot the Pianist!

Some years ago the Society for Theatre Research gathered information for a gazetteer of all theatres in England in existence before 1912. This led to an exhibition entitled 'Curtains'. As a young historian involved in this project I was enthralled. A gift of old theatre programmes has since brought the memories flooding back. Apart from the actual lists of plays and players these relics contain interesting messages and advertisements.

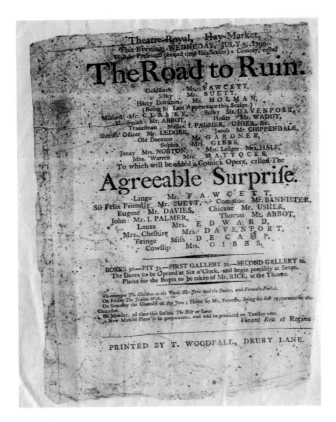

An old theatre handbill from the Theatre Royal, Haymarket, London.

Some of the attractions on offer shown on a programme from the Opera House, Winter Gardens, Blackpool, 1902.

In those closing days of the last century catering was in the hands of people eager and willing to meet clients' needs: 'breakfasts, dinners and teas at every hour'. One proprieter near Manchester's Palace Theatre was proud to offer 'a marble hall and restaurant with Herr Weltermann's Blue Hungarian band and a six course dinner for two shillings and sixpence'. The range of services offered by tradespeople seemed boundless. The chemist would provide a full set of dentures for 20 shillings and Zom Palatin fixative for holding them firmly in place 'to avoid embarrassment'. If you needed a pair of spectacles you went for an eyesight test to a chemist of jeweller. A broken umbrella frame could be repaired at the barber's shop.

Beguiled by romantic plays, cathartic performances or stirring outbursts of song, theatre-goers must have been thought fair game. Adverts ranged from a soap that dispelled blotchy skin to vibra massage for curing deafness. One remedy for baldness and 'scurvy' (sic) – (he must have meant scurfy or dandruff) was made from a 'receipt' of Queen Catherine of Hungary. The Hungary Water Man would 'attend patients at home for five guineas plus expenses'. He charged one guinea for a visit to his consulting rooms.

From theatre programmes came the alarming information that a revolver could be bought for seven shillings and sixpence, the same price as a hot water bottle. A Webley or Colt was thirty shillings while big-game rifles cost three pounds and upwards. Perhaps this is the origin of the old saying 'Don't shoot the Pianist. He's doing his best!' Mark Twain said they were expendable in the Wild West!

By the twentieth century theatre programmes advertised Zeima gas lamps and Royal Ediswan carbon and electric lamps 'to illustrate homes'. Elocution lessons were becoming fashionable to cure shyness, lack of confidence and 'negative thoughts'. Before 1910 when Trade Unions were using advertising, one poor chap was depicted as being turned down by his intended. 'No, Charles,' she cries dramatically, 'it can never be. I find your hat does not bear the Hatters' Trade Union Label.'

Prices were interesting too. A Marcel Wave was only one shilling and sixpence. A lady's tailored suit from Moss Brothers could be bought for 31/2 guineas, an 18 carat gold half-hoop ring with five diamonds for 42 shillings, Humber bicycles from 8 to 19 guineas. Cycling was the 'in' thing!

But what of the performances themselves? One Blackpool charity concernt for the theatrical profession featured 67 different turns from 11 theatres and palaces of variety. In heavy type it stated: 'Encores cannot be allowed.' No wonder! Let's hope it wasn't 'twice nightly'. Artists had to work hard.

Among the sheaves of programmes I was of course particularly interested in my own area. Fleetwood's Albert music hall, built 1863 and still standing, in North Albert Street, was turned into a furniture repository.

A signed photograph of 'Nipper Lupino Lane', son of Lupino Lane, the well-known star of film and music hall.

Gladys Cooper, beauty of the early twentieth-century music hall.

Only its cast-iron pillars serve now as a sad reminder of Edwardian and Victorian Music Hall days. Twenty years after its opening, Mr J. Wearden, Manager, advertised 'An entirely New Company, Messrs Alexander and Payne'. Artists included negro comedians and champion skaters; the sisters Wallace; burlesque artistes and dancers; skipping rope dancers; Mr Granville, comedian; Tute's Great Ministrels, the largest and best troupe now travelling; clever comedians; splendid tenors; deep and powerful basses; and 'the best solo violinist in the world'. No negative thinking here! Modesty gets you nowhere and it could have been true. Prices were two shillings or sixpence. 'Carriages to arrive by 10.15'.

On 8 May 1874 the Fleetwood Choral Unions Concert was held in the Albert Music Hall. Originally a cotton warehouse built by millionaire Benjamin Whitworth, it had been made redundant by the American civil war and consequent cotton famine. Instead of cotton bales it became filled with people and laughter. The grand opening comprised 'a great musical entertainment followed by a dramatic representation of Bardell v. Pickwick' from which the proceeds went to the Deserving Poor at Christmas time. Popular songs of the day included 'O Had I Jubal's Lyre', 'O Ravishing Delight' and most appropriately for that wild December night in Fleetwood 'What Are the Wild Waves Saying?'

A Grand Concert on Friday 10 February 1882 to raise money for the Parish Church Enlargement Fund brought eminent artistes from Manchester: Madame Laura Howarth; Miss Dutton; Seymour Jackson. Besides bringing down the house, it also raised the roof, for as The Lost

George Royle's Fol-de-Rols, c. 1920.

Miss Lily Hanbury photographed by Percy Guttenberg of Manchester in 1907. Guttenberg was a contemporary of my father, Clement Houghton.

Chord was being 'rendered' a volume of water descended upon the audience. This was mildly commented on by a reporter on that rainy night as 'inconvenient'.

By 1900 the Queen's had been entirely repaired, redecorated and fitted with electric light. Seats ranged in price from sixpence to one guinea. A well-known Fleetwood public figure, farmer John Crookall, was such a theatre lover he had two seats made into one to accommodate his large girth. The Queen's was advertised by Harry Osmond, Manager, as 'the Popular Palace of Pleasure'. Gus Elen, who enjoyed shooting holidays in the Fylde, appeared there, as did Arthur Haynes and George Formby Senior. By the 1960s the Palace was empty and falling into decay, its tottering proscenium a sad comment on the death of live performances and the limelight.

In the hours I spent with these programmes it took but little imagination to evoke the rapture of audiences transfixed by such great singers as Enrico Caruso, Dame Clara Butt, Madame Patti and other ghosts from a brilliant theatrical past: Martin Harvey; Mrs Campbell; Vesta Tilley; Henry Irving. Sooner or later Blackpool billed all the great names.

In mind's eye the heavy, gold-swagged, ruby, velvet curtains swished, twinkling light caressed gilded cupids and cherubs with golden harps poised on boxes and proscenium. Opera glasses were trained with an air of expectancy; ostrich plumed fans rustled; opera cloaks fell to the floor unheeded and the sound of wild applause was like the surging of the sea.

Exchanging such thrills for 'the box' was not a good idea.

CHAPTER TWENTY-THREE

'The Promenaders' Joy'

Lytham St Annes Pier Ladies Orchestra

The parents loved the music. I admired the long white satin dresses worn by the ladies in the orchestra. More than a hundred years ago the celebrated bachelor scholar Dr Poole, Lytham resident and tutor to de Vere Clifton of Lytham Hall was writing about the local pier; 'The promenaders' joy, the popular centre with its splendid Pavilion in the midst of the waves'.

Lytham Hall, ancestral home of the Clifton family.

The single-screw steamer Brigg *was built by Lytham Shipbuilding and Engineering Co. for J. Holt & Co. of Liverpool. It was launched on 20 July 1909.*

The learned doctor when not composing poems or studying documents relating to the ancient Cell of Lytham was apt to enthuse about the vista: 'the ever-moving panorama of ships, steamers and small craft – across the estuary is Southport glistening like a jewel, to the left broad meadows, wooded hills and hollows with white homesteads'. He loved Lytham and may well have been among the 800 strong crowd who witnessed the dramatic grounding off the sandhills of that magnificent steamer *Huntcliff* in 1894.

Easter Monday 1865 was one of Lytham's greatest days. From Preston and beyond special trains brought in a multitude. Friendly Societies carrying silk banners, excited children, townspeople and dignitaries all gathered in Market Place to be led by the band of the Third Lancashire Militia. In grand procession they headed for the new pier where Lytham Volunteers formed a guard of honour for Mrs Clifton who stepped from the Assembly Rooms to declare the 900 feet iron structure well and truly open.

Apart from the stormy night of 6 October 1903, when two sand barges drifting before the gale sliced the pier in two and that disastrous night in

1928 when it was almost entirely destroyed by fire, the pier was indeed the promenaders' joy but the jewel in its crown appears to have been the Ladies Orchestras.

'To walk for exercise' on the pier was a mere twopence in old money! If you brought baby in a 'bassinette' that was fourpence and grandad in a bath chair (of which there were plenty in Lytham) cost sixpence.

From the jubilant reports of old residents it was a happy, musical pier, home every midsummer to one of the finest musical festivals in the North of England which attracted top performers. The continuing tradition however was for ladies orchestras. As early as 1910 Kate Earl and twelve lady musicians gave concerts.

We were on the Pier every night in the twenties to listen to the Ladies Orchestra. We would be waiting at the door for the caretaker to unlock, going early so that we could be sure of our favourite seats on the front row. Mine was number 4 which gave me the best view of my favourite lady,

St Annes-on-Sea, 1908. Under the management of Mr W.H. Nutter, the pier became popular for its musical entertainment, including Mr Dallas and his Troupe and Mr Carlton and his Pierrots. Crowds were 'capitally entertained' in 1904 in the new Moorish Pavilion which seated 1,000 people. Russ Conway, Claude Hulbert and Leslie Henson all performed there. Hourly pleasure trips were run from the jetty at the end of the pier to Liverpool, Morecambe, Fleetwood and Lytham.

Mr William Rees (centre), late of Hallé Orchestra fame, was the conductor of the St Annes Pier Orchestra in 1937.

Doris Bellinghall, who played the clarinet. The conductress was Clarice Dunnington. Her sister played the cello and her husband, Archie Glenn, the oboe. He visited twice every season. Other ladies were Victoria Shakespeare on trumpet and Madame Eva Martin, violinist. Clarice had three lovely evening dresses which she wore on stage and the ladies would have a sly bet as to which she would be wearing for a particular concert. Her *pièce de resistance* was a long velvet gown.

During the winter, Clarice led a small ladies orchestra at the exclusive Manchester store, Kendal Milne.

The picturesque setting of the Floral Hall where the ladies played, surrounded by plants and flowers was left unharmed but literally 'in the waves' when Lytham Pier was cut in two. The damage caused by the disastrous fire, however, was irretrievable and the once beautiful pier became a rusting eyesore. A vigorous campaign raged to pull it down and eventually in 1960 it was demolished.

The Ladies Orchestra lived on, performing in the Moorish Pavilion of the St Annes Pier, opened in 1885 by the Hon F. Stanley. Lytham joined with St Annes on Charter Day, 1 May 1922, Councillor C.F. Critchley being the Mayor of the new Borough. Patrons remember Miss Anne Hunter's Orchestra of Ladies and the delightful café nearby which served teas, ices and minerals. St Annes Pier also had a Floral Hall designed by Mr E. England in which the Ladies Orchestra played.

The pier toll was increased to three old pennies (two for children) but no extra charge was made for the orchestra. Performances were daily at 11 o'clock in the morning and eight o'clock each evening. Sunday 14 September 1930, witnessed a special concert when Mr W.N. Jacklin was vocalist.

By 1932 Mr William Rees, once a member of the famous Hallé Orchestra under John Barbirolli, was conductor of Lytham St Annes Ladies Orchestra, Henry Whittaker being lead violinist. The ladies were still presenting 'Popular programmes of light holiday music played with good taste' on 13 August 1939 scarcely a month away from the declaration of the Second World War which was to annihilate for many a carefree existence.

Talking to the few residents who still recall those joys, Gladys Youles, Dorothy Wordsworth, Helen Harrison, Edwin C. Johnson, Brenda B. Bughes, one savours with a pang, happy times past in a less complicated world where Pears' soap cost fourpence ha'penny and a fur-trimmed winter coat could be had for five pounds in present day currency. Hey ho! for the pier and what was voted 'The best concert on the Fylde Coast'. Ladies take a bow!

CHAPTER TWENTY-FOUR

Those Daring Young Men in their Flying Machines

O ne of the most vivid impressions that has remained with me all my life was the sight of the airship R101 flying over Blackpool during our annual holiday in the 1930s. To a ten-year-old, got out of bed specially to watch, it looked like a great silver sausage against the moon.

England's first aviation week, held at Blackpool in 1909. Here we see a Voisin biplane. A.V. Roe introduced a daily air service which flew passengers from South Shore, Blackpool, to Southport and Manchester.

A souvenir postcard of the first aviation meeting in England, which was held at Blackpool in October 1909.

Some thirty years earlier, as it had done on many occasions, Blackpool surprised the rest of Britain by arranging an airship flight from a site near the Gasworks. Stanley Spencer reached a height of 1,000 feet and flew 26 miles in an airship 75 feet long driven by a petrol engine on 20 October 1902. With flying now commonplace, it is difficult to conjure up the hardship and danger faced by earlier aviators who risked life and limb in their most basic craft.

Until 1909 aerial excitement for visitors to Blackpool had been limited to Stansfield's Patent Aerial Flight at the Fairground, but this was the big one, Aviation Week on the Fylde Coast from 18 to 23 October. With real men and machines, this was spectacularly different. Father was there of course, with his friend Willie Turnbull. The excitement and novelty, like that of 'Foudroyant', stayed with him for years.

From early Monday morning Lytham Road was thronged with immense, enthusiastic crowds, motor cars, bicycles, landaus, wagonettes and tram cars all surging towards Squire's Gate. By noon when the machines were brought out of their sheds 18–20,000 people were on the ground. It was a truly historic occasion. Had not Doncaster beaten Blackpool by three days it would have been the first Air Pageant to be held in Britain. However, Blackpool's was the first to involve insurance cover for airmen and spectators and to be sponsored by the Aero Club.

Five British aviators were competing: Singer, Row, Charter, Mortimer and Neale, but the experienced French team were the big attraction. Mr Henry Farman, an Englishman brought up in France, had lost his machine in transit from Berlin. M. Leblanc had a Blériot monoplane, but the first to try his wings was M. Rougier. 'The hind wheels did just leave the ground but the aeroplane did not get into the air before the engine stopped.' Henry Farman, the world's distance champion, borrowed M. Paulhan's Voisin biplane and had the honour of being first in the air, rising 40 or 50 feet. Turning towards St Annes he was forced to alight after only half the circuit 'owing to some slight defect', but tools were brought and he tried again, completing the full circuit to the sheer amazement of the crowd.

The first Lancashire man, Mr A.V. Roe, with a brave attempt in Bulldog No 1, travelled 100 yards but failed to take off. As he pulled up in good style, the crowds scrambled out of his way. He decided that he needed smaller propellers. Mortimer, another Englishman, described as a 'dark horse', was perhaps the airman who fell into the sea at St Annes. Older residents remember wading in to his rescue. Though they 'nothing common did or mean upon that memorable scene', the Britishers did not cover themselves with glory as at Waterloo.

Some of the Frenchmen did better and scooped all the prize money. M. Henri Paulhan made a magnificent flight at 3.30 pm; M. Rougier remained in the air for almost half an hour and Leblanc got the best from his machine for a brief space in atrocious weather. In fact throughout the five days it had been so wet and windy that flags had to be flown from Blackpool Tower indicating whether or not flying was in progress.

Picture postcards in their thousands were sent home by visitors who had thronged Blackpool for this unique occasion. One from 'Rose' read: 'We are having a nice time. By Jove, it is full here today!' She and her friend had seen the Frenchman M. Fournier perform in an Antoinette monoplane and a Farman biplane. All subsequent events such as Sir Alan Cobham's Air Circus were recorded on picture postcards. Such interest generated what came to be known as 'flying fever' and picture postcard scenes were superimposed with couples in aeroplanes flying over the Tower and captioned 'Having a high old time in Blackpool'. Morecambe, Southport and Fleetwood followed suit.

The following year a second flying meeting, 'The Blackpool Flying Carnival', was held at Squire's Gate. On this occasion Claude Grahame-White, the first Englishman to be granted a British certificate of proficiency in aviation, flew around the Tower and on to the Isle of Man. History was made when for the first time an aeroplane carried mail to the island and again in 1931 when W. Hamnet, a North Fylde Farmer, sent 2,000 chicks from Blackpool Airport to Roumania. In 1909 Grahame-White had founded the first British flying school in Paris and later helped in establishing Hendon Aerodrome.

It was the persistence of A.V. Roe, following his disappointment at the Blackpool Air Pageant, that earned success and ultimate glory. Some years

Talbot Square and North Pier, Blackpool, as it looked in the early years of the twentieth century.

My friend Fred Woods first specialised in light planes for glider work. He is seen here working in his uncle's sail loft at Fleetwood seventy years ago. He later worked for Marconi and became Mayor of Chelmsford.

later he introduced a daily air service to Southport and Manchester, taking off from the beach at South Shore. Built by A.V Roe and Company, which he founded, the Avro Anson was a familiar sight at Squire's Gate in pre-war days, but it is the Lancaster bomber for which he is best remembered.

Among these great names, let's not forget Fred Woods, son of a Fleetwood printer, who was one of the few people in the country experimenting with sustained flight at the turn of the century. He constructed his aeroplanes in a sail loft and transported them by ferry to Over Wyre where he made practice flights. The long suffering ferryman used to wink at his passengers and say: 'Well, you know they dropped Fred and he cracked his head on the slopstone.' This bright young lad, however, went on to design direction-finding equipment for Marconi and twice became Mayor of Chelmsford. I am proud to say that Fred and I became good friends, corresponded for years and occasionally met at the North Euston Hotel, Fleetwood. Today's trans-continental supersonic flights seem a far cry from half-hour hops in primitive machines with hand cranked propellers at the start of the century, but we should not forget that such progress stemmed from the courage, ingenuity and foresight of those pioneers who personified the old maxim: 'If at first you don't succeed, then try, try and try again.

CHAPTER TWENTY-FIVE

Wrea Green, a Village in the Domesday Book

It was the restoration of Wrea Green Windmill, some twenty years ago, that first sparked my interest in the history of a charming village. Dr Jonathan Ward was then the owner and he too was very interested, bringing about a wonderful reconstruction of the imposing tower mill by employing local craftsmen, the families of whom had worked in the area for generations.

A typical carrier's cart, c. 1900.

Cricket is played on the village green at Wrea Green. Feeding the ducks is still a popular pastime at this pond, which stands on the largest of the Fylde's traditional village greens.

The grinding stones with their time-honoured carved incisions designed to regulate the milling of corn and produce fine or coarse flour were transformed into a garden table, built into paving or left leaning and picturesque amid lush greenery.

There is an interesting record in 1860 of one component which had been in use at Wrea Green mill and 'Was taken to the grand old lady of Lytham', in other words to the windmill on Lytham Green. Inscribed were the words, 'This is the upright shaft. It has done its work for 150 years.'

The windmill at Wrea Green resembled other towers in the 'Cornfield of Amounderness' and was known as a smock mill, the tower being topped by a smock-like wooden cap.

North west villages like Wrea Green which nowadays have become both prestigious and commuters' delights were isolated communities 200 years ago and had to be mainly self-supporting. Strangers were regarded with suspicion but the itinerant pedlar with ribbons and laces, the carrier's lumbering cart from Preston with supplies of paraffin – these were welcome. They also brought news and juicy gossip.

Pot-holed lanes, dusty in summer and muddy in winter were walked or ridden on horseback until bicycles came in. The nucleus of the hamlet consisted of church, inn, clusters of thatched white-washed cottages and the village green with its duck pond and pump so Wrea Green remains, in some ways, a perfect stereotype, further enhanced by having the largest village green.

The village pump at Wrea Green.

The windmill and manor house stood somewhat aloofly apart. The lord of the manor owned the mill and farmers were forced to use it for getting their corn ground. For this enforced privilege they paid tolls and were also expected to fire watch; fire was a great hazard if winds changed direction and the windmill sails ran wild to produce sparks flying into thatch. There is record of the four-storey windmill's sails turning in 1770 at the village now called Wrea Green.

In 1860, a steam engine was installed. Sign of progress but not a good idea, it caused a boiler explosion and the mill being set on fire. The damage led to the upper storey becoming a pigeon loft and the interior of the mill a storehouse by 1900.

Cottages and farms dated back to the sixteenth century, low-built to resist winds, but brilliant against dark green fields of oats or the gold of ripening corn. Homely sounds such as the creaking of windmill sails, the blacksmith's ringing hammer, the clopping of horses' hooves, children playing, poultry clucking and quacking – in the daily round and common task, these were then background noises. Villagers at Wrea Green worked hard but there were compensations: pace-egging at Easter, mummers and carol singing at Christmas midsummer and autumn bonfires, Collop

Mr Lancaster of Wrea Green on his penny farthing. His mother was crowned one of the May Queens on a Club Day.

Monday and pancakes on Shrove Tuesday. There was dancing on May Day and at harvest home in the big barn to the tune of a lively fiddle. Fiddlers were in demand.

Wrea Green was known in monastic days at Ribby with Wrea and in the Domesday Book put together by William the Conqueror's Commissioners as Rigbi. Villagers paid tithes to the prior of Lancaster. Nearby Singleton had to do the same in colts, lambs, pigs, wheat, cheese and butter. Those monks lived well!

In 1297 Richard de Wrea lived at Rigbi. Vestiges of his ancient manor house which was sited on the Green were used as a cottage after Ribby Hall, home of the Hornby family, had been built. Manor cottages in Bryning Lane possibly derived their name from the old manor connection.

Close your eyes, sniff the air – lanes are sweet with hawthorn blossom white as snow, the gorgeous aroma of freshly baked bread made from Wrea Green windmill flour and the scent of roast pork is issuing from open cottage doors. . . . Among rare trips to Wrea Green, a family favourite was calling at The Grapes, known as Dumpling Inn because of the annual feast of dumplings held there. Run by the Noblet family for generations, John had a prize-winning greyhound christened Likes Ale. As youngsters we

The Grapes Inn, Wrea Green. Notice the block steps alongside the modern litter bin. These were for mounting your horse in the days when the Grapes was nicknamed the Dumpling Inn.

were only interested in the home-made lemonade on a hot June day. It was a great place to run about and 'play ball', besides feeding the ducks which since those days have increased so greatly in number, they are becoming a problem.

CHAPTER TWENTY-SIX

Post Horn Gallop

Garstang's Glory Days

Queen Elizabeth's Charter of 1597, renewed in 1679, appointed 'eight honest and discreet Garstang men' to run their (even then) ancient market town. Saxons and Romans had settled there, the Scots burned it down, and Cromwell's troops occupied the houses on the west side of the High Street. During the rebellions of 1715 and 1745 large members of the Pretenders' troops 'reclined in the sun under walls of houses in Garstang'. Bonny Prince Charles himself was said to have rested on the steps of the Cross.

Garstang market place, c. 1900.

There was always plenty going on in the way of such alarums and excursions, but the average Garstang resident, working hard on the farm and going to market every Thursday, took little notice. Items of news were cosy rather than stirring: 'On Easter Monday 1820 occurred the first meeting of children to trundle eggs at the Bridge Inn Field, Lancaster. Among 2,000 children indulging in the innocent recreation 100 came from Poulton and Garstang.' Three days later came the Stallion Show at Garstang. 'The inn and public house keepers of the town gave a silver cup for the best horse.'

And there you have it! The innkeepers played such an important part in the life of the town in the eighteenth and nineteenth centuries. Garstang was well known in coaching days as it lay on the main route from London to Edinburgh. These same influential men fought against the coming of the railway as they enjoyed a lucrative trade, supplying horses and catering for travellers.

Of thirteen inns in the town the most important and the principal posting house was the Royal Oak. By the 1840s, when its popular landlord was Mr Dobson, twenty-four coaches a day passed through Garstang, the first at 7.30 a.m., the last at midnight. Horses were stabled in a large yard behind the inn and at a busy place in Green Lane, known as 'Little Rochdale', which employed many stable hands. Provender for the horses came from the corn mill on the River Wyre. The poor exhausted beasts were rubbed down fed and watered, and then changed over for another team.

At the inns a special 'snug' was kept ready for the passengers, who quickly ate, drank and refreshed themselves as schedules were tight and no dawdling allowed. Second in importance was the Eagle and Child, but with market days also to cope with, all the High Street inns were busy: the Blue Anchor; Golden Ball; Red Lion; Holy Lamb; Shovel and Broom; Farmer's Arms; and the Crown, formerly called the Swan. The King's Arms had a large stabling area at the back and Henry Huntingdon's Wheatsheaf Inn in 1900 ran a handy little shop.

James Lewtas, a Garstang boy training in Liverpool to be an accountant, wrote to his parents: 'I shall travel by the Invincible to Garstang on Saturday next.' Such romantic names singled out the coaches: North Briton; Regulator; Brilliant. Names like Tantivy, Tally Ho, Dart, Comet and Quicksilver were indications of their speed. Because of the cracking pace maintained by the coaches mishaps did occur. On 20 October 1828 the North Briton was upset near Carnforth owing to the breaking of a pole. Most passengers escaped with bruises but one young woman was severely injured. At Scotforth a child was killed. The approaching coach could be heard miles away by the sounding of the long post horn, a signal to watch out and prepare. Mothers scooped children and chickens off the street and rushed them indoors to safety; landlords roared instructions. The hurtling coach and horses, driven relentlessly by coachmen defending their reputations for speed, slowed down for nobody. It was a point of honour that the mail must get through.

Mr Prescott Bigston, American millionaire, on a tour of England. He is seen here changing horses at the Eagle and Child at Garstang on 28 June 1911.

Coach drivers faced all weathers. On one occasion the driver of the Bath mail coach found his tall beaver hat frozen to his head. The landlord, it is said, poured hot water round the rim to loosen it. 'Hot toddy' was waiting at the counter the moment the coach driver strode in. Many were heavy drinkers and some earned a reputation for being drunk in charge. Snow was the worst enemy. Sometimes a coach could be stuck in drifts for days. In 1825 a coach en route to Garstang was blown over and in 1817 one crossing 'Lancaster sands' was overturned by a sudden gust of wind, two horses were drowned; the coachmen and nine passengers were drenched.

This was a time of fierce competition between coaching firms. 'March 1 – opposition has started in the coaching trade. Thomas Gregson and Co. having commenced running the Royal Liverpool against J. Dunn and Co.'s Royal Telegraph.' Dunns were charging only half the price that Gregsons were asking. In 1803 Smith, Bretherton and Co. had charged two guineas inside and £1 6s outside for 'the only regular coach to London from the King's Arms and Continental Inns, Lancaster'. It was all highly organised and if the Flying Machine drawn by six horses with postillions astride the two leaders took three days to get to London from Kendal, Garstang was not going to be left behind.

Many renowned passengers were carried in these coaches. Sir Walter Scott, the novelist, who stayed overnight at the Royal Oak, Garstang, forgot his two breast pins, 'one with Walter's and James's hair, another a harp of Irish gold, the gift of the ladies of Llangollen'.

Charges and Rules governing the Turnpike Roads also affected the running. On 23 February 1823, 'at a meeting of the Trustees of the Garstang and Helring Skye Turnpike Road it was agreed to make two diversions by which Galgate Brow to the south and Buckstone Hill to the north might be avoided'.

So, pause to think when you next view the handsome 200 years old Royal Oak. Look closely at the stone mound guarding the corner of the inn on Church Street. Those deep scorings gouged into the stone were made by iron-clad wheels when twenty-four coaches a day clattered over the cobbles in and out of Garstang.

CHAPTER TWENTY-SEVEN

On the Rocks

I was never a dedicated rock climber, rather more of a 'hanger on', if you will excuse the pun. Although not, in my young days, a sufferer from vertigo, the discomfort of aching limbs driven over and over again to new effort when early energy had already been expended, did not appeal to this hedonist. Dewdrops dripping from the nose end, wet clothing clinging to shrinking limbs, these things militated against the sport, although I did experience the joy of wet-scented greenery bruised by crampons, grass, fern, heather and the like all around, of moss caught under questing finger nails along pitifully narrow ledges, of the sheer grittiness of millstone grit under the palms, moist wind on the face and on the up and up, the sound of water falling far below. After several attempts at a girdle traverse, I clung to the spirit of the sport rather than to the letter. While my brother and his companions sweated alternately with heat and fright I found myself a convenient sheltered ledge and painted the scene. On this same ledge on one occasion we all crouched during a thunderstorm, watching with fascination the blue lightning sparking and bouncing from the metal hairpins of one of our party. Thus, rock climbing for me became essentially a spring and summer pastime, but vividly I remember my last attempt before discovering, most sensibly, my true metier.

We had decided to spend a New Year's Day on a line of low 'cliffs' and though it was cold, the slate and stones were dry so we set off from Stonethwaite. However, within the hour soft, persistently fine drizzle began, the type of rain that when set in seems to go on for days. Nevertheless we continued, passing not a soul in the swirling mist. Our clattering boots stormed over rocky outcrops, drenched through dubs, doused in oozy peat hags, squelched sedge and sucked tussocks. Through springing heaths and slippery skirtings of snagging furze and whins, at long last we reached our goal. We were wet, yes, we were wet, but we set about what we had come to do in the way that only young people can. Came the meal break, 'Where's the sandwiches?' asked my brother Edward, whose heroes were Eric Shipton and Edward Whymper.

'You should have them,' I said heavily. The air, besides being misty, became suddenly blue as brotherly insult was hurled in my direction. Our two companions nobly shared their butties, but we were left half empty rather than half full.

From 'on the rocks' to Brighton Rock! Here I am (left) with my flatmate Winifred.
We both worked for Surrey County Library but enjoyed, at weekends, catching the
Brighton Belle, a train journey which took only one hour and was quite inexpensive.

Napes Needle, Lake District. In our teens we explored the Lake District widely, climbing Great Gable, Esk Hawes, Green Gable, Red Pike, Haystacks and Coniston Old Man. Edward and friends Alan Clixby, George Coates and Brian Dilworth, having climbed the Wetterhorn, were in a mountain hut in Switzerland when war was declared in 1939. They descended to find every visitor gone. The British Consul took them overland by car to Paris en route home.

The last climb of the day found me deeply dispirited and I withdrew shiveringly. The final pitch took far longer than expected as all three were tired and hungry and we left the rock face amidst silence and approaching darkness. The paths were now muddy rivulets and the sedges shuddering quagmires of despair. Looking back on it, I think we must have all been mad. In the darkness far ahead a tiny pinpoint of light moved steadily towards us and eventually a man clad in oilskins, carrying a hand lamp arrived. 'What on earth are you doing out on a night like this?' he said, shaking raindrops around like a shaggy dog. He was a water bailiff and had to be out whatever the weather.

Two years earlier my sister and I had a similar experience trudging Honister Pass in a snowstorm. The men at the slate quarry asked us the same question. It was around Christmas time and we were allowed to shelter and rest up a while in a hut, where I suspect they kept the dynamite. Those workmen were equally astonished and must also have

Coniston was in Lancashire when we had a week's holiday in this LMS camping coach in 1937. What a revelation to see clean sparrows and clear water running in the becks! Each morning the friendly station staff brought a locomotive up the line carrying cans of water – our daily supply. It chuffed alongside in a fury of steam, stopping by the carriage door. Another revelation!

thought us mad, but I shall never forget, on that occasion, before the storm had blown up and the dusk approached, those wondrous blue shadows in the gullies of Haystacks and on the snow fields of Robinson.

At last, very tired and gently stewing in our own juices, since the rain had stopped and a warm, wet wind had sprung up, we reached Rosthwaite. All doors were closed; a few lights behind curtains or blinds were showing, but the village had a deserted, call-tomorrow look.

Suddenly, all four of us stopped in our tracks, roses lifted to the wind, all in the same direction, like the famous Bisto Kids of that now long ago advertisement. A delectable smell wafted towards us, causing our empty stomachs to rumble and lurch drunkenly as the gastric juices overflowed. It was the smell of freshly baked bread. Like the famous kids (Ah! Bisto), we allowed the odour to permeate our nostrils. Breathing in deeply, we followed the trail round a corner and into a tiny court where stood an open door ablaze with rosy light from within. The heart-warming odours drifted from a great, black, glowing fire oven.

'I haven't got much,' said the cheerful soul in charge. 'The bread is still in the oven, but I have some steak pies left over from lunch. I've a few pasties too and there's plenty of hot tea. Don't sit there in wet clothes. Take your coats and jackets off. It's warm in here with the oven on. Get a wash at the sink. There's soap and a roller towel . . . it will do for all of you.'

Absorbing warmth, relaxing weary muscles, basking in glow, we perched on wooden stools, taking in the satisfying ambience of a Lake District kitchen, steadily munching and drinking tea in huge, white mugs decorated with blue bands. The world was a wonderful place and we would not have missed our outing for the world – now it was over! 'I like to see good appetites,' said our Borrowdale benefactress. 'Wouldn't go on t'tops myself, but some do well off it. Are you sure you wouldn't like another fill-up?' Indeed our thirsts were unslakeable.

It must have been the steak pies and the fruit pasties of this guardian angel that settled me thereafter for the good life rather than the quivering quagmires of the high fells. To the four winds of heaven went the rope, the crampons and tricounis in exchange for the perfume, the flowers and the candy. To this day, however, I never pass through Rosthwaite without thinking of Mrs Towers, her second-nature kindness, common sense, cooking prowess, rich Cumbrian accent and sparkling Mr Pickwick spectacles. There is involved even essential Wordsworth:

> She was a phantom of delight
> When first she gleamed upon my sight.

Within a few months of that outing, the last we had together, Hitler marched into Poland, without a by your leave, and our world was never the same again. It was the end of childhood.

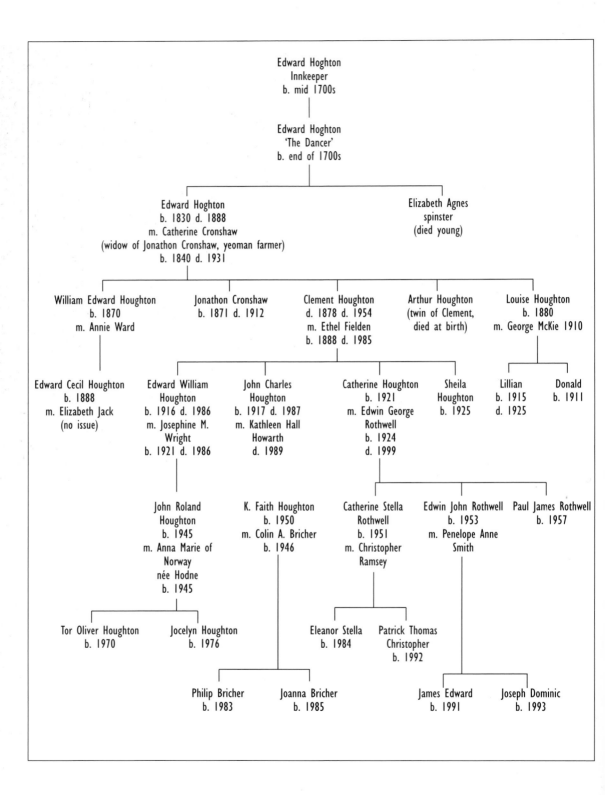